Reading as if for Life

Reading as if for Life
Spirituality for Booklovers

David Dickinson

The Lutterworth Press

The Lutterworth Press
P.O. Box 60
Cambridge
CB1 2NT
United Kingdom
www.lutterworth.com
publishing@lutterworth.com

Paperback ISBN: 978 0 7188 9817 5
PDF ISBN: 978 0 7188 9818 2
ePub ISBN: 978 0 7188 9819 9

British Library Cataloguing-in-Publication Data
A record is available from the British Library

First published by The Lutterworth Press, 2025

Copyright © David Dickinson, 2025

All rights reserved. No part of this edition may be reproduced,
stored electronically or in any retrieval system, or transmitted
in any form or by any means, electronic, mechanical,
photocopying, recording, or otherwise, without
prior written permission from the Publisher.
(permissions@lutterworth.com).

To Yvette
with thanks for everything as always

Contents

Acknowledgements		ix
1.	Introduction	1
2.	The Beginnings of a Spirituality of Reading	5
3.	Reading Charitably	23
4.	Circling the Text	44
5.	Self-Identity and Reading	61
6.	Silent Conversation with the Absent Other	71
7.	Giving Texts Holy Attention	85
8.	The Beauty of Books	102
9.	Contemplative Reading	119
10.	Escaping the Net	139
Bibliography		149
Index		153

Acknowledgements

The work of a critic is honest and honourable work, but it does feel secondary in that music critics depend on composers, drama critics on playwrights, and literary critics on authors. Without the original works there would be nothing to comment on. I must therefore express my indebtedness to the writers whose work has stimulated my thinking, only a small proportion of whom feature here. They have informed my preaching, my teaching, my writing and, not least, this book.

Thank you also to all at Lutterworth Press who have finessed *Reading as if for Life*, especially the copy editor, Dorothy Luckhurst, and Sarah Algar-Hughes with whom I have been in most direct contact. I was especially pleased that Georgina Melia picked up on my reference to Guiseppe Arcimboldo and used it to design such an eye-catching cover. It has been a joy to work with all at Lutterworth again.

1

Introduction

In the early chapters of *David Copperfield*, the young boy found consolation in 'reading as if for life'. His recently widowed mother had married Mr Murdstone, who brought with him his over-indulged daughter, and introduced such cruel changes to the household that the young David was increasingly alienated from his beloved mother. In a chapter entitled 'I Fall into Disgrace', David is in no doubt that he would have been driven mad by his new family situation were it not for the fact that Murdstone had left undisturbed a small room at the top of the house, next to David's bedroom. David had the key to this room, which housed a small collection of books his biological father had kept. It was as if no one except for David even remembered the room was there. The books he read in the room he escaped to were mainly, but not exclusively, eighteenth-century novels. These filled the imagination of one of the best-known, nineteenth-century, fictional characters. He tells us that they were his coping mechanism in hard times:

> From that blessed little room, Roderick Random, Peregrine Pickle, Humphrey Clinker, Tom Jones, the Vicar of Wakefield, Don Quixote, Gil Blas, and Robinson Crusoe, came out, a glorious host, to keep me company. They kept alive my fancy, and my hope of something beyond that place and time, – they, and the Arabian Nights, and the Tales of the Genii, – and did me no harm; for whatever harm was in some of them was not there for me; I knew nothing of

it. It is astonishing to me now, how I found time, in the midst of my porings and blunderings over heavier themes, to read those books as I did. It is curious to me how I could ever have consoled myself under my small troubles (which were great troubles to me), by impersonating my favourite characters in them – as I did – and by putting Mr and Miss Murdstone into all the bad ones – which I did too. ...

This was my only and constant comfort. When I think of it, the picture always rises in my mind, of a summer evening, the boys at play in the churchyard, and I sitting on my bed, reading as if for life.[1]

This is one short, sad scene depicting a period of loneliness within a childhood of mixed fortunes and yet, within it, we see Dickens's faith in literature's ability to keep alive a hope of something beyond the here and now. Reading was no guilty pleasure for the young reader, but a lifesaver. For the boy David, reading was not escapism, but something that permitted him the flights of fancy and imagination that kept him sane. He was weighed down with great sadness and loneliness, yet he found new friends in the people he met in his father's books. The little room he called 'blessed' was like a sanctuary for the boy. This was 'reading as if for life'.

In a later novel, Dickens gives reading as if for life another expression. In *Hard Times*, the brutal Thomas Gradgrind enforces intolerable working conditions on his factory employees. After long hours of hard labour, the workers go to libraries to read. There:

[t]hey wondered about human nature, human passions, human hopes and fears, the struggles, triumphs and defeats, the cares and joys and sorrows, the lives and deaths of common men and women! They sometimes, after fifteen hours' work, sat down to read mere fables about men and women, more or less like themselves, and about children, more or less like their own. They took De Foe to their bosoms, instead of Euclid, and seemed to be on the whole ... comforted by Goldsmith.[2]

---

1. Charles Dickens, *David Copperfield* (Ware: Wordsworth Editions, 1992), Chapter IV.
2. Charles Dickens, *Hard Times* (London: Penguin Classics, 1995), Book 1, Chapter VIII.

This was not an escape from life's hardships, nor an avoidance of reality, but the means by which these badly-done-to workers learnt to cope with their unfortunate lot. The workers read to have a life other than work. They read in order to make sense of their hard lives.

What Dickens suggests in *David Copperfield* and *Hard Times* is only the beginning of what reading as if for life can mean. Reading as if for life, as a tool in the practice of spirituality, can mean making a journey towards the enlightenment that results from an encounter with God, by either emptying oneself before the text, or finding oneself through the text, or engaging in a silent conversation with the absent Other, or paying holy attention to the arts through close reading, or appreciating the beauty of reading for pleasure, and thus apprehending the God who is Beauty. In this way, reading is capable of making us better, more moral, people and liberates us from our restricted selves into the pure air of thankfulness, like David Copperfield, dreaming ourselves into the world beyond. Note, please, that I say 'is capable of' because these are not inevitable results of reading.

The reading of which I write here is the reading of serious secular literature other than the scriptures and other than intentionally spiritual texts. In other words, this book is primarily about reading novels and poetry as a spiritual exercise. In some chapters, poetry will be the focus when poems are more accessible for discussion. The Dominican writer, Chris McVey reminds us that in the book of Exodus anyone who wished to consult God went to the meeting tent outside the camp (Exodus 33:7) and suggests that we continue to meet God outside the camp, outside the institution of church, outside the formality of church documents. 'It is', he said, 'outside the camp that we meet the Other who is different – and discover who we are. And where our "home" really is.'³ The Hebrew Scriptures' allusion to a meeting place 'outside the camp' is especially significant for Christian spirituality when we remember that Jesus died outside Jerusalem, on a waste tip known as Golgotha, feeling abandoned by God. There, 'outside the camp', heaven met earth perhaps as never before. The spirituality of reading described in this book takes us beyond the sacred literature to which Christian believers customarily turn when they want to meet God; it takes us outside that camp to secular literary fiction. I am convinced that we shall find that God is also there.

---

3. Quoted in Timothy Radcliffe, *Alive in God: A Christian Imagination* (London: Bloomsbury, 2019), p. 274.

I am sometimes teased that my academic interest in religion and literature is little more than an excuse to read novels. Perhaps it is, on occasions! Those who tease me in this way may well be people who regard reading novels as a guilty pleasure. I resist the suggestion that reading fiction is a form of escapism, but I do acknowledge that it takes us to other places. As Emily Dickinson said in a poem I remember, 'There is no Frigate like a book / To take us Lands away.' My aim, therefore, is that this spirituality of reading will provide and explain a number of reasons for reading secular literature which are more noble than simply to while away a few pleasurable hours, not the least of these reasons being that reading literature can lift us into godly realms. Outside the camp there is a meeting place where we meet God.

2

The Beginnings of a Spirituality of Reading

In the early days of the pandemic crisis of 2020, Daniel Defoe's *Journal of a Plague Year*, a fiction published in 1722, probably based on his uncle's diary which had recorded first-hand experiences of the 1665 plague, sold remarkably well in the United Kingdom. The journal, a first-person narrative purporting to be the journal of a Whitechapel saddler, recounts the curious effects of fear and anxiety on the behaviour of a population dreading an awful death, including the diary-keeper's regret that he had been careless and had not stocked up on necessities. Later, he stockpiled flour, malt for brewing, butter and cheese, yet was never confident that this was the right thing to do. He witnessed instances of appallingly callous behaviour, as fear reduced some of his fellows to a dog-eat-dog mentality.

In Britain in 2020, fear and anxiety also had an immediate impact on how people behaved when coronavirus threatened the way of life we had previously enjoyed. Some behaviour caused by the pandemic was irrational: in the early days, panic buying resulted in empty shelves in supermarkets, especially in the spirits, wine and beer section, with the weird exception of Corona beer. Other behaviour was more easily understood. Weeks of staying at home except for essential business increased some people's spare time, while others, who had to try to adjust to working and educating children from home, had less free time. The pressures of inactivity and hyperactivity changed much for many. One change was a turn to religion: at one point it was said that over ten per cent more people watched online worship during the lockdown than usually attended church in the good times. Was this because more people found they had spiritual needs, or was it because watching an online service took less effort than attending church in the good times? Another change was in reading habits: as bookshops closed for lockdown they reported a remarkable increase in sales, most notably a 45 per cent spike in sales to people in the 18- to 24-year-old age group. More will be said about reading habits later, but, for now, the question on my mind is whether there was any link, other than coincidence, between these two effects of a crisis that transformed our culture, lifestyle and economy. Did, and does, reading feed spirituality? Why might I feel close to God with literature not only when *in extremis* but also whenever I engage with the best words in the best order, the beauty of a well-crafted story, a well-written passage of prose or the aesthetics of language? Is it because God dances across the page uninvited, or is it because I look for this in my reading? In this book I intend to explore the relationship between spirituality and literature, and to encourage religious believers to read literature other than sacred texts for spiritual enrichment. This is a *spirituality* of reading; and I must begin by sharing with you the assumptions about spirituality that lie behind my thinking. They are not especially original but they lay the ground for my reading of the literature I refer to here.

Spirituality is a slippery concept, generally agreed to be difficult to define and sometimes seen as a woolly substitute for traditional, institutional religion. In contrast with hard doctrine and rigorous dogma, spirituality is regarded as soft and lacking academic rigour. Whereas the study of theology is rooted in authoritative texts, reason, experience and established tradition with repeated tests to distinguish heresy from orthodoxy so that no one strays far from what is claimed to be true, spirituality can seem to roam free, linked to not much more than what we think about what we experience. However, this is an unfair caricature of an important feature of religious faith. It is better to think of spirituality as theology-in-practice or lived theology. Theology can be studied as a purely academic subject but being a theologian involves more than being an academic. It involves being a theological person who thinks with theological tools and behaves in a manner based on theological principles. Theology is only complete when it is studied as a faith. Studying theology leads to doing theology and being theological. This means that theology always has a practical aspect; it is lived. Spirituality cannot, therefore, be set apart from theology, but is that aspect of theology that helps people study religion as faith. In this regard, spirituality is what reminds theologians that the object of their otherwise purely intellectual quest to know, or at least find God, is unattainable because God is the mystery beyond our imagining and the perfect Other beyond our imperfect knowing. Spirituality is associated with mysticism and takes us to the edge of mystery and the limits of human language. We cannot deny that theology and spirituality need each other to keep each other grounded: spirituality prevents theology from being merely theoretical and unhinged from experience, whilst theology prevents spirituality from veering away from centuries of human faith. Theology offers criteria by which we can evaluate spirituality, and vice versa. Some thinkers see this relationship as mutually interactive, whilst others attribute priority to spirituality because it reminds theology of its spiritual core. I see the study of spirituality as a discipline that prevents us from merely doing theology in an academic way; it underscores our efforts to be theologians, by which I mean that what we study has become part of who we are.

University prospectuses reveal that in recent decades the academic world has often tended towards interdisciplinary studies, no longer inclined to separate one pure discipline from another. Blurred boundaries between subjects rather than hard edges have become the norm in the human pursuit of meaning and understanding. What I explore in this book is another example of this trend, for I am, in effect, hosting a conversation between spirituality and literature, the latter a traditional purely academic discipline and the former less distinctive. We shall discover that spirituality is unavoidably in dialogue with several other disciplines, including ethics. We shall also find that our spirituality is always informed by its context in culture, which is the *locus* in which human experiences take form and find expression. For these reasons, I argue that novels and poetry can be in fruitful dialogue with spirituality for they, too, often address deep matters of meaning and belief, in the context of the culture in which we hold our beliefs and exercise our religious faith.

This argument relates to my growing conviction, based on over three decades as a Methodist minister working closely with people in all manner of circumstances, in sadness and in joy and, most recently, in the extreme and discombobulating societal reaction to a new coronavirus, that humans are essentially spiritual beings.

As Cottingham in his philosophical essay on the soul said, it is a commonly held view among those who philosophise on the nature of humanity that it is 'of the nature of a finite creature to reach for the infinite'.[1] Whether or not we affiliate ourselves to any organised system of religious belief, we naturally think and behave spiritually; we reach out for something beyond ourselves that we cannot grasp. Although the concept of the soul is neither scientific nor orthodoxically Christian, some truth remains in the notion that human beings have souls. Souls are the essence of our being; they are who we are; they are what make us persons and individuals. I, therefore, want to be liberal in my working definition of spirituality for the sake of this book because, by being less definitive, we shall discover elements of spirituality in the practice of reading that might otherwise remain hidden. We shall find that reading is a satisfying food that replenishes the soul. We shall find a varied menu. Not all in this exploration will be to everyone's liking. What will offend the taste buds of one diner will delight another, and vice versa. Sauce for the goose may not be sauce for the gander!

My conviction that we are spiritual beings predisposes me to the idea that spirituality is something that flows through our religious impulses and experiences, as well as through our psychology, our social and political lives and our physical sensibilities, as Daniel Coleman describes it.[2] He sees spirituality as a driving force that looks beyond and outside ourselves in longing to be meaningfully connected to humankind and creation. It propels our imagination and connects and binds us to ourselves, the surrounding world and the divine. Spirituality is both our response to our awareness that we are creatures to whom life is a precious gift, and a generative inner longing that pushes us onwards and outwards. Following Ronald Rolheiser, Coleman says the beginning of our sense of spirituality is the recognition of our individuality, seeing whatever it is that has made us what we are. We progress from this initial awareness to aligning, and finding a place for, our unique individuality within the wider social and created order. Understanding spirituality in this way makes it more than an inner feeling or a psychic state because it is

---

1. John Cottingham, *In Search of the Soul: A Philosophical Essay* (Princeton, NJ: Princeton University Press, 2020), p. 133.
2. Daniel Coleman, *In Bed with the Word: Reading, Spirituality, and Cultural Politics* (Edmonton: University of Alberta Press, 2009), p.8.

The Beginnings of a Spirituality of Reading

always attentive to the direction and impulses of the world beyond our minds and hearts. For Coleman, spirituality is thus to do with the way we live out our lives in relation to the environment, other people and our hidden selves.

In his introduction to a collection of essays in which novelists reflect on their craft, Paul Fiddes defines spirituality as the reaching out of the whole person towards realities that transcend our senses.[3] This reaching out often involves certain practices of prayer such as contemplation, meditation and mysticism. Some consequently assume spiritual practice is nothing more than an alternative phrase to describe a believer's prayer life. Spiritual practice usually includes a discipline of stillness and receptivity of mind akin to that of the reader sitting book in hand. Such stillness makes one aware of 'the mysterious reality of love and justice'[4] and takes one on a journey of moral transformation. This journey heads towards the divine 'out there' and the God within, otherwise known as the 'true self'.[5]

One of the great classics of spirituality, one which has accompanied me in one way or another since my days in theological college, is what some regard as one of the earliest examples of autobiography, a classic of spiritual life-writing, Augustine of Hippo's *Confessions*. The young Augustine, who eventually became bishop of Hippo and one of the most influential theologians of all time, was famously converted to Christianity as a result of an invitation to read. He was also the first to develop a theory of reading, which merits attention in the early stages of this book because any spirituality of reading, in one way or another, builds upon this giant's foundations. He was the first to regard reading as a spiritual exercise.

Augustine's conversion to Christianity while reading in a Milanese garden in August 386 was one of two highlights in his life which associated reading with mystical experience. The second of these highlights came in the autumn of the following year in Ostia, the seaport of ancient Rome, and was part of one of the last conversations he had with his dying mother, Monnica. Experiences like these – a conversion and a final parting – are formative for most people. Few of

---

3. Paul Fiddes, ed., *The Novel, Spirituality and Modern Culture* (Cardiff: University of Wales Press, 2000), p. 11.
4. Ibid., p. 12.
5. Nancy M. Malone, *Walking a Literary Labyrinth: A Spirituality of Reading* (New York, NY: Riverhead Books, 2003), p. 3.

us forget when we became committed to our faith and conversations with dying parents are cherished for ever. Such experiences have lasting effects on one's thinking. This was so for Augustine also. He recounted them in his spiritual autobiography, *Confessions*, which he began to write in 397.

The better known of the two experiences is the mystical experience that resulted in Augustine's conversion from his early interest in the Manichee sect to orthodox Christianity. Two years previously, Augustine had become professor of rhetoric in Milan where one of the first people he visited was Ambrose, its bishop. He was a cultivated scholar fluent in both Greek and Latin, and well-versed in ancient and modern theology. Augustine, out of interest in Ambrose's oratory, went to hear Ambrose preach and found himself impressed. It seems that Augustine was already becoming sceptical about Manicheism, a scepticism that grew as he listened to a wise old presbyter named Simplician telling him the story of an eminent Roman orator-philosopher named Marius Victorinus. Study of the Bible had attracted Victorinus, a pagan by birth, to the Christian faith and he became a secret Christian. Offered a clandestine baptism to hide any embarrassment, he declined and went public. Augustine could easily see why Simplician told him this story: it was to advise him that he, too, should not be ashamed to lay aside the religious philosophy he had followed to that point.

Meanwhile, Alypius, a former student who became a life-long friend, another friend from Carthage named Nebridius, and his mother Monnica joined Augustine in Milan. *Confessions* gives the impression that by now there was a small coterie of young Africans in Milan with Augustine, each with great expectations and far-reaching ambition. Augustine, however, was not in good spirits. In fact, in August 386, Augustine felt very disturbed, describing '[his] inner self [as] a house divided against itself'.[6] There was a small garden at the house where he lodged which his absent host allowed him to use. Augustine reports that the tumult in his breast had become so oppressive that it drove him into the garden where, accompanied by Alypius, he hoped no one would interrupt his fierce inner struggle. He speaks of a great internal storm that bursts forth as a deluge of tears. At this point he chose to leave Alypius so that he could weep

---

6. Augustine of Hippo, *Confessions* (Harmondsworth: Penguin, 1961), 8.8, line 1.

The Beginnings of a Spirituality of Reading

to his heart's content, believing that tears are best shed in private. *Confessions* book eight, chapter twelve tells of Augustine slumped beneath a fig tree wrestling with existential questions mainly to do with his overwhelming sense of sin. These reached a nadir in suicidal thoughts as he asked himself why he should not put an end to his ugly sins at that very moment.

Then, from a nearby house, he hears the singing voice of a child repeating again and again, 'Tolle lege', which translates from Latin as 'Take it and read it.' Because he cannot identify this refrain as being part of any familiar childhood game, he interprets this as a divine instruction to pick up a Bible and read the first passage on which his eyes fall. Having rushed back to join Alypius, with whom he had left his copy of Paul's epistles, he reads part of Romans 13:13-14 and feels his confidence restored and doubt dispelled. Alypius is also aware of the mystery and wonder of this shared experience and they hurry to tell Monnica, who is overjoyed because her son now stands 'firmly upon the rule of faith'. According to book nine, chapter four of *Confessions*, in the weeks that follow, Augustine and his saintly mother often walked in the villa garden reciting psalms.

By the autumn of the following year, Augustine had left his post as professor of rhetoric and was set on returning to Africa. However, while he and Monnica waited in the quiet port of Ostia for a ship, their plans were scuppered because civil war broke out and the sea was closed to all shipping. Matters worsened when Monnica became seriously ill with a fever. In her heart she knew she would not survive. Indeed, she lived only nine more days. Nevertheless, she died content, because she had lived to see her son baptised and she felt ready to say her *Nunc dimittis*.[7] In the final days of Monnica's life, a second auricular mystical experience helped Augustine to accept her death and cope with his grief. He and his mother were alone, leaning out of a window overlooking the courtyard garden of the house in Ostia in which they were staying. They shared what he calls a serene and joyful conversation, in which they speculated about the nature of the eternal life of the saints. 'We', Augustine says, addressing God as he does throughout *Confessions*, 'laid the lips of our hearts to the

---

7. Henry Chadwick, *Augustine of Hippo: A Life* (Oxford: Oxford University Press, 2009), p. 38.

heavenly stream that flows from your fountain.'[8] Then he describes a sublime moment of spiritual ascent:

> As the flame of love burned stronger in us and raised us higher towards the eternal God, our thoughts ranged over the whole compass of material things in their various degrees, up to the heavens themselves, from which the sun and the moon and the stars shine down upon the earth. Higher still we climbed, thinking and speaking all the while in wonder at all you have made. At length we came to our own souls and passed beyond them to that place of everlasting plenty, where you feed Israel for ever with the food of truth. There life is that Wisdom by which all these things that we know are made, all things that ever have been and all that are yet to be. ... And while we spoke of the eternal Wisdom, longing for it and straining for it with all the strength of our hearts, for one fleeting instant we reached out and touched it.

This fleeting instant, or flash of thought, brought them in touch with the essence of their very beings as well as into an awareness of the timelessness of God, but it lasted only momentarily and they returned to the mundane sound of their own speech with all its limits and imperfections, bound as human speech is in a fallen world governed by time. What has happened in this mystical experience is that Augustine and Monnica have moved both upwards (beyond all material things towards God) and inwards, entering and, at the same time, transcending their minds, until they find themselves in 'a region of unending abundance' where past and future have lost meaning, 'a realm of pure mind'.[9] This great mystery brings Augustine to a point of self-understanding in relationship with the divine. In short, this mystical experience has brought him close to God. This informs the theory of reading which emerges in Augustine's extensive writing in later years, which describes reading as a spiritual exercise requiring

---

8. Augustine, *Confessions* 9.10, line 14.
9. Brian Stock, *Augustine the Reader: Meditation, Self-Knowledge, and the Ethics of Interpretation* (Cambridge, MA: Harvard University Press, 1996), p. 118.

'a critical step upwards in a mental ascent'.[10] We shall see that such mental ascent is not exclusively intellectual – we do not only learn from reading – but the process of reading can be, for us, a step upwards in *spiritual* ascent. Reading is a spiritual exercise.

    Augustine's experiences in Milan and Ostia share some common features. Both involve courtyard gardens; in Milan, a child's voice rings out through a window, while in Ostia mother and son look through a window to the garden below. These auricular mysteries give Augustine a sense of the divine image as one which is perceived from the material world through the opened barrier of a window, from which the visionary can look into the spiritual realm of Eden. As the poet George Herbert said,

> A man that looks on glass
> On it may stay his eye;
> Or if he pleaseth, through it pass,
> And then the heav'n espy.[11]

    Augustine's literary output was vast. Over 500 sermons, 113 books and treatises and more than 200 letters survive. The most substantial are *City of God* and *Confessions*, both of which have had an abiding influence on Christian theology and spirituality. *Confessions* gives us a strong impression of the importance of reading in Augustine's education. This had begun in the town of his birth, Thagaste, where he received pre-baptismal religious instruction, although his baptism was indefinitely postponed because he became seriously ill. Later he studied in Carthage and developed a love of philosophy, opening up for him a career as a teacher of rhetoric. He learnt from Ambrose's sermons that scripture is not to be read for its literary sense, and this proved to be an early step on his road towards conversion. Augustine carefully spelled this out: 'While all can read [scripture] with ease, it also has a deeper meaning in which its great secrets are locked away. Its plain language and simple style make it accessible to everyone, and yet it absorbs the attention of the learned.'[12] The deeper meaning of which he spoke is uncovered through contemplation and interpretation, requiring a form of spiritual reading. Throughout

---

10. Ibid., p. 1.
11. George Herbert, The Elixir, stanza 3.
12. Augustine, *Confessions* 6.5.

his writings Augustine reflected further on this concept of spiritual reading and, as a result, he developed what is thought to be the first ever theory of reading.

We should note that, as far as Augustine was concerned, all his thinking about reading was underpinned by his doctrine of the Fall. He argued that we resort to reading because since the Fall, personified in the expulsion of Adam and Eve from Eden where they had enjoyed direct communication with God, God has not spoken directly to humankind. As fallen creatures, we can no longer hear God's word directly, but must be satisfied with reading God's reported word. So we see that Augustine's theory returns again and again to the Fall and is coloured by his awareness that we are fallen creatures. There are several features of Augustine's theory of reading I feel it is important to highlight.

The first aspect of his theory for us to note is the relationship between silent and spoken reading. In book six, chapter three Augustine remarks on Ambrose reading silently so that 'his heart searched into the sense, but his voice and tongue were silent'. Contrary to the popular misperception which assumes that Augustine was astounded to see Ambrose reading silently because this was a phenomenon he was observing for the first time, Augustine's comment that he never saw Ambrose reading in any other way than silently emphasised not the novelty but the peculiarity of Ambrose's practice.[13] He was also stressing that this was Ambrose's customary practice. According to Steven Roger Fischer's history of reading, this is the earliest instance of a distinction being drawn between loud and silent reading. Because only a handful of passages in antiquity attest to the practice of silent reading, Fischer concludes that Augustine remarks on what he saw because it was 'surprisingly rare'.[14] Daniel Coleman argues that Augustine was disappointed when he found Ambrose reading to himself, because he had hoped to start a discussion with his senior, perhaps interrupting at some point to ask the scholar a question. After all, it was a scholar's job to read to students and congregations.[15] On the other hand, Stock points out that there were very good reasons for Ambrose to read in silence, the main one being the need to conserve

---

13. Ibid., 6.3.
14. Steven Roger Fischer, *A History of Reading* (London: Reaktion Books, 2003), p. 90.
15. Coleman, *In Bed with the Word*, p. 47.

his weak voice for preaching and the other being a desire to keep curious onlookers, such as Augustine, at a distance so that his study was not disturbed. There was an additional reason why reading aloud was the norm, and that is that it was more congenial when reading unpunctuated scrolls and codices. Without punctuation, often the words needed to be sounded for the reader to get the rhythm of the prose and find its sense. For these reasons, seeing someone like Augustine enjoying strolling around the villa garden with his mother while reciting psalms would have been a much more common sight than seeing a solitary individual reading with motionless lips.

We can understand for ourselves why reading out loud suited readers of that time by turning either to the final Penelope section of James Joyce's *Ulysses*, over forty pages of unpunctuated text, with only a few paragraph breaks, or to Bernardine Evaristo's 2019 novel *Girl, Woman, Other*, where full stops are used only at the end of chapters. Either can, of course, be read silently but the artistry of their writing and the text's meaning sing out more if they are read out loud. The converse also makes the point: a speaker, say an orator or a preacher, when preparing a speech may test the words' ability to convey the intended meaning, by sounding out the script as it is being written. I do the same: as I write a sermon, I can hear the words internally and, at important turns in the passage, if I become animated and forget myself, I might become audible.

The second aspect of Augustine's theory of reading is to do with aesthetics. In *De musica* Augustine discussed the practice of rests in musical performance, as well as in the reading aloud of texts. In any well-composed song, of the modern era as well as ancient times, intervals between notes add to the impression of a pleasing whole in the way that shadow throws prominent features into relief in a painting.[16] Music is about silence as much as it is about sound. In any piece of music, the spacing between the notes matters as much as the notes themselves. John Cage's *4'33"* may be an extreme case that proves the point. It is four minutes and thirty-three seconds of music in which the performer sits silently before a silent piano. Is it music? Is it silence? Perhaps it is neither or both! Performed well, it is just over four and a half minutes of careful listening to the sounds around us. Similarly, words on a page make sense because of the spaces between them. Speech uses silence, while silence involves

---

16. Stock, *Augustine the Reader*, p. 7.

interior speech. Speech also incorporates intervals of silence which provide space for interpretation, or, as Stock expresses it, silence 'is emptied of outer, physical sound so that it can be opened to inner, permanent knowledge'.[17] When the text becomes an object of aesthetic appreciation and contemplation, the act of reading becomes a form of meditation, which is a valuable tool for achieving a sense of God. What happens is that reading concentrates the reader's attention so that the normal flow of time, measured by the passing sound and letters, is replaced by an extensive present 'distending' thought which creates an illusion of permanence. Augustine argued that to achieve this state of transience, the reader must jettison all linguistic and literary corruptions caused by our innate fallen self-centredness. We must lose ourselves before the text.

Third, Augustine was the first to propose that a relationship is established when a reader sits before a text, a relationship between the sender, the receiver and signifiers, where meaning is created out of the sounds and letters of a word. We might think of this as the thickness of words. Poets such as David Jones, Seamus Heaney and Michael Symonds Roberts have warned about the meanings of word being thinned out and language being less substantial as spiritual and theological connotations have been lost in the secularisation of contemporary culture. The examples Roberts cited in a radio programme broadcast on BBC Radio 4 were the words 'water' and 'wood', which any poet would have once been able to use sure in the knowledge that readers would pick up images of baptism and the cross of Christ. Now, with the emptying out of theological meaning from our vocabulary, the words have lost this significant depth and poets have to forge new metaphors to express the depth and wonder of human experience. Augustine proved this point many centuries previously as part of his philosophy of reading. In *De doctrina Christiana*, he cited the story, told in Exodus 15:25, of Moses throwing a tree into some foul water at Marah to make the water sweet and safe for consumption. Here, he says, a word referring to an object as 'wood' can be understood simply as wood or as signifying something else if it has symbolic, figurative or metaphorical extension. In this instance, the wood of the tree is more significant than mere wood; it also signifies divine healing and purifying power. According to Augustine, this shows that words can have a transformative function, allowing the reader to make a

---

17. Ibid.

The Beginnings of a Spirituality of Reading 17

transition from one level of understanding to another. He extends this notion by referring to another biblical passage, this time in the New Testament where, in the Vulgate which was Augustine's Bible, Paul uses the word *bos*. Ordinarily this signifies an ox which, according to the law of Moses should not be muzzled when treading out the grain, but when Paul uses *bos* in 1 Corinthians 9:9 he is referring figuratively to a preacher who should not be muzzled when fulfilling his calling. The word moves from what Augustine calls 'proper' use, or literal sense, to 'figurative' use. He compared this to the way the soul gives rise to a person's vitality, and was beginning to unpack the depth of meaning in words. He was moving towards arguing that words can carry human and divine intention. Being fallen creatures creates a problem, though. It is that our understanding is so limited by our fallen nature that we can never be sure that we are interpreting divine intentions in words correctly. For Augustine, therefore, careful contemplation and study of scripture was key to the pursuit of wisdom. Indeed, it was a crucial route.

He saw human existence as a ladder of levels of being, whose summit, the object of our aspiration, is the high point of absolute repose and changelessness. At the lower levels of human existence, we feel a ceaseless desire for upward movement, at each step making an improving change, until we reach the equilibrium of being one in oneself and one with God. The soul's upward movement within a fallen world can be seen as either a return to or an imitation of harmony and unity.

Fourth, following on from this notion, Augustine developed a philosophy of language related to the human consciousness of time. He discussed this extensively in book eleven of *Confessions* beginning with his explanation of the first chapter of the book of Genesis which, he said, indicates that before creation there was no time. The creation of time was part of the act of creation. Time becomes problematic when it is part of human consciousness. Time is more complicated than we expect: for instance, I wrote some of this book during the lockdowns to counteract the Covid-19 pandemic of 2020, when each day felt long, yet the weeks passed quickly. Did time fly or did it drag? In a similarly strange way, Augustine argued in *De quantitate animae*, that time bore some relation to the way we assimilate language when reading. The example he used was the word 'Lucifer' whose meaning cannot depend only on the length of time it takes to pronounce the syllables since its signification survives after the sounds cease to be heard. Augustine's deeper point was that the language of scripture is eternal because it represents divine speech, yet also temporal because it is written on parchment. When we read, our task is to discern both the divine and the human sense of language, both the plain and the figurative, the profound and the superficial, the literal and the spiritual sense of literature.

Fifth, Augustine's theory of reading finds roles for will, memory and inspiration. Thinking about the intentions of words, Augustine considered how our mental intentions are expressed in words that are exposed to the possibility of varied, even adverse, interpretations. Because, as fallen creatures, Augustine thought of humans as being no longer in direct communication with God, he recognised that we cannot know with certainty what God's intentions are. As a result, there can often be a profound disconnection between what we think and what we do, as well as between what we see on the page and how we understand what we read. Nonetheless, God's will for us is demonstrated through our innate desire to know God and this leaves open the possibility that scripture offers the reader something through which God's will, by our use of memory and the gift of inspiration, can be internalised and directed towards good actions. In the case of memory, we should note, as Stock says, that as hearing differs from listening, and seeing differs from looking, so memorising is not the same as remembering. For Augustine, memory springs from a combination of mental action and linguistic intention. Before I speak or write, an understanding of what I want to say fills my thoughts, then as I speak or write mental images of the original idea serve as my guide and form my words. Of course, in his innovative spiritual autobiography, Augustine gave memory a critical role in developing self-knowledge. He was discontented with merely reliving a past episode; instead, he sought to put his recall of past events into a schema which gave sense, meaning and purpose to the life he recorded. His auricular mystical experiences in Milan and Ostia, and the divine and spiritual significance he attributed to them, serve as outstanding examples of this. As Stock says, for Augustine, memory was the basis of human culture, which includes the language, literature and institutions of people, their beliefs, customs and rituals.[18]

All this relates to the sixth aspect of Augustine's reading theory, which is the role of inspiration to bridge the gaps between reader and

---

18. Ibid., p. 13.

3

Reading Charitably

Writing alone in my book-lined study, I am in the company of friends. My friends here are the novels stacked on the shelves behind and to the right of me. They did not all begin as friends. Of some, I was highly suspicious before I met them. Most of these novels are now arranged alphabetically by author, with three exceptions. After Z for Zola, I have a shelf for novels whose authors rewrite biblical stories, a remnant from a previous research interest;[1] a second section displays novels which depict the British Methodist Church (I find I have an illogical sentimental attachment to this collection, perhaps because some of them are rare copies, but also because this is the Christian denomination I have served for more than 35 years);[2] and a third more haphazard section is an unsorted compilation of recently read novels, filling odd corners because sorting them among the alphabetised collection now seems hardly worthwhile. The existence of this last section testifies to one of the bibliophile's most difficult issues: how to make space for books. To have the moveable shelf stacks you find in library store rooms would be a luxury of which I can only dream! Getting rid of a book to make space for another hurts, because a book one has read has become a friend. Its ideas,

---

1. See David Dickinson, 'Lest the story be lost: Biblical Fiction' in Stephen Prickett, ed., *The Edinburgh Companion to the Bible and the Arts* (Edinburgh: Edinburgh University Press, 2014), pp. 104-113.
2. See David Dickinson, *Yet Alive? Methodists in British Fiction since 1890* (Newcastle upon Tyne: Cambridge Scholars Publishing, 2016).

its characters, its philosophy and its author have, at the very least, a small part to play in your life. A book, once read, occupies a small folder in your memory files. You may not have agreed with or enjoyed all you read in the book, but you can never be sure when a future random thought or incident will remind you of the novel and make you want to turn to it once more. Breaking up (a library) is hard to do. But, as I prepare to retire from active ministry and move from a manse to a smaller home, I must face this challenge.

Many books have become my friends over the years, and one of the first points I want to make about the spirituality of reading is that there is much to be gained by fostering friendliness towards books: regard the book as your friend. Not all Christians have done this. For instance, beginning in the 1880s, James Potts, the long-serving editor of the *Michigan Christian Advocate*, conducted a decades-long campaign against reading novels. The *Michigan Christian Advocate* is an independent publication for and about United Methodists in the state of Michigan, which began as a paper publication in 1874 until it moved online in 2010. Potts was its first editor and he remained in post until 1912. His was perhaps the most prolonged and vituperative campaign against novel reading, but it is far from unique. The lasting effect of such campaigns is that some Christian readers retain a remnant of suspicion about novels as a potentially misleading or even corruptive influence on their lives.

Potts's editorials, bearing titles such as 'Decadence in Literature' (1884), 'The Dime Novel Curse' (1894), 'Satan's Newspapers' (1894), 'Beware of Corrupting Fiction' (1901), 'Filthy Fiction Will Wreck Any Life' (1907) and 'The Moral Hurt of Novel Reading' (1908), argued that one of the pernicious effects of novel reading was that novels morally corrupted readers and caused crime and disorder. He argued that the young, who were not yet fully trained in the discipline of Christian living, were especially vulnerable to the corrupting influence of novels. He expressed the wish that those who wrote, published and sold unwholesome literature could be reached and punished, because the damage they inflicted on the young people of America was a crime worse than the opium trade forced upon China or the liquor trade in Africa. Parents were, therefore, warned to monitor the books their children were reading. Potts's campaign was not a carte-blanche campaign against all novels, but he did engender suspicion of most fiction. The Detroit Conference of the Methodist Episcopal Church recorded its concerns about the corrupting influence of novels in its Minutes of 1885. These compared the 'pernicious character and tendency [of fiction to be] to the mind and morals of the innocent and unsuspecting what slow poison is to the body'.[3] The Conference believed that fiction insidiously caused moral decadence and personal devastation. In the following year, another Potts editorial claimed that novel reading weakened the intellect and contributed to 'silliness'. A mind crowded with one exciting tale after another lived in a state of 'novel-drunkenness'.[4] Such concerns were not new in America. They followed the earlier example of the third American President, Thomas Jefferson, who had declared he would never allow his daughter to read a novel. Why, Potts wondered, nearly two hundred years after Jefferson, would novelists not make a hero of a 'robust, square, uncompromising, intelligent, and triumphant Christian' such as he?

In Britain, others had similar thoughts. In 1955, the Reverend Dr Leslie Weatherhead wrote a letter of appreciation to the novelist Howard Spring after he had published *These Lovers Fled Away*. Spring's fame rested on a 1940 novel about a Methodist politician, *Fame is the Spur*, whose story reached the wider public in 1947, when Boulting Brothers made a well-received film of the book starring Michael Redgrave. Weatherhead, a prominent and popular preacher who attracted large crowds at the City Temple in London, used his letter to Spring to express appreciation of the earlier novel, then concluded with a suggestion:

> I wish you would write a novel and make a parson the hero – and why not a Methodist parson, for were you not once a local preacher? Parsons are so often effeminate asses, or they commit suicide or they are stupid or obscurantist in modern fiction. The doctors always shine but the poor parson so rarely is a he-man and I know so many grand fellows.[5]

---

3. Quoted by Matthew T. Herbst in '"The Pernicious Effects of Novel Reading": The Methodist Episcopal Campaign against American Fiction 1865-1914', *Journal of Religion and Society* 9 (2007), pp. 1-15; p. 5.
4. Ibid., p. 6.
5. Quoted in Marion Spring, *Howard* (London: Collins, 1967), p. 177.

More famously, the testimony of the British novelist, Jeanette Winterson, first in fictional form in *Oranges Are Not the Only Fruit* (1985), then in the form of memoir in *Why Be Happy When You Could Be Normal?* (2011), is that her adoptive mother, Mrs Winterson, a fiercely conservative Christian, encouraged Bible reading before all other reading. She did not exclude fiction entirely. Mrs Winterson's favourite 'non-Bible book'[6] that she read to the young Jeanette over and over again was *Jane Eyre*, but it was only when Jeanette read it for herself that she discovered that Jane did not marry St John at all but returned to marry Rochester. Mrs Winterson had rewritten the ending so that it better fitted her own understanding of Christian discipline and moral behaviour.

Such antipathy towards secular fiction had previously paved the way for writers such as the Hocking siblings – Josiah, Silas and their sister, Salome. Silas was a Methodist minister who was the first novelist to sell a million copies of one title in Britain. His books enjoyed phenomenal popularity, especially *Her Benny*, his 1879 account of street children, who had been abused by their parents and were now selling matches for a living. This was based on his first-hand experiences as a minister in Liverpool. All three siblings wrote didactically, and were unashamedly propagandist in their promotion of Methodist ideals. Christians keen to read novels that were wholesome and safe could rely on the Hockings.

This demand for Christian novels had also opened up a market for Charlotte Maria Tucker, who, from 1852 until her death in 1893, wrote prolifically for younger readers under the *nom de plume*, A.L.O.E. Her books, in which her aim was to encourage support for the Victorian Evangelicals' campaign to preserve the Protestant identity of England and its Established Church, were often awarded as Sunday School prizes. In the late nineteenth and early twentieth century distrust of secular fiction also created a vogue for biographies of missionaries and of biblical figures. Tucker also wrote many of the latter, notably focussing on Hebrew women whose narratives she foregrounded from their near hiddenness within the patriarchal text of the Old Testament.

In the United States, it also had the unexpected consequence of encouraging writers such as Stephen Crane and Upton Sinclair to

---

6. Jeanette Winterson, *Why Be Happy When You Could Be Normal* (London: Vintage, 2011), p. 73.

turn to specifically Christian characters and settings for their novels. The assumption upholding these trends was that novels could do some good, but that more often than not they were dangerous and could cause harm. As a character in W.D. Howells's novel, *The Rise of Silas Lapham*, said, 'The novelists might be the greatest help to us if they painted life as it is, and human feelings in their true proportion and relation, but for the most part they have been and are altogether noxious.'[7]

The Church has, therefore, always needed to reflect on the place of non-Christian literature in the Christian life. The debate about the value or otherwise of secular literature has variously heated up and cooled down throughout the centuries. The Church has often discussed what significance it should attribute to the poems, stories and philosophies of the pagan world. Most famously in the early years, in relation to the relative authorities of secular and religious powers, Tertullian asked, 'What has Athens to do with Jerusalem?' Jerome adapted Tertullian's question into a three-part literary question which paid particular attention to literary genres, 'What has Horace to do with the Psalter? Or Virgil with the Gospel? Or Cicero with the Apostle?'[8] In the first of these questions, Jerome compared secular poetry with the lyrics of the psalms, in the second, he compared heroic narrative with the tragi-comedy of the Jesus narrative, and, in the third, he compared two forms of forensic rhetoric.

Reading widely has supported me spiritually in many ways, and the breadth of that reading has included readiness to read texts that might be regarded as atheistic or non-Christian. Readiness to do this could be justified by the words of St Paul in his letter to Titus: 'To the pure, all things are pure' (1:15, NRSV), or 'To the clean, all things are clean.' Not that I regard myself as pure – or clean! However, I take Paul's statement to mean that the pure heart and the clean mind are beyond being corrupted, and that the faithful disciple will not be lured away from the straight path. This contrasts with Jerome's word of caution that we should not drink simultaneously from the

---

7. Quoted as an epigraph to Herbst's article, '"The Pernicious Effects of Novel Reading"', p. 1.
8. Jerome's *Epistle 29*, quoted in David Lyle Jeffrey, *People of the Book: Christian Identity and Literary Culture* (Grand Rapids, MI: William B. Eerdmans, 1996), p. 76.

cup of Christ and the cup of demons.[9] Nonetheless, it is in keeping with Jerome's defence elsewhere of his use of non-Christian authors in his own writing. Jerome's argument was, first, that the Hebrew Scriptures made abundant use of gentile literature and their authors adapted the techniques and styles of secular writers, second, that the New Testament continued this practice, with St Paul quoting from Epimenides in his letter to Titus 1:15, Menander in 1 Corinthians 15:33 and Aratus in Acts 17:28 (although without attributing the quotations), and, third, that classical literature in similar ways had continued to influence the Church's apologetic, catechetical and theological writings since the time of St Paul to his own day.[10] Therefore, he could, too.

What matters to us when navigating our way through this dilemma is that we read with care. The clean mind and pure heart will not be in peril when reading the novels Potts hated so much if the books are read carefully and judiciously. In this respect, we can find a guide for our spirituality in Alan Jacobs's theology of reading, and much of what I say in this chapter is informed by Jacobs's thinking and applies it to my own spiritual and theological practice. Jacobs's starting point is Christ's law of love for God, neighbour (whether friend or foe) and for self, which, because it is called the greatest of all commandments, is intended to govern all things. He reminds us that the fourteenth-century English spiritual writer, Richard Rolle, intimated that love was proved in three areas of the believer's life – in thinking, talking and working. Our thinking includes our reading, talking includes writing, and both reading and writing are forms of work. The thought given to preparing this book, the writing of it and the work of producing it should similarly be directed and governed by love.

Jacobs refers to the Aristotelean idea that love produces knowledge, and to the Augustinian claim that only those in whom the double love of God and of neighbour is built up when reading the scriptures has truly understood that the Bible shows how central to the exercise of textual interpretation is the role of love. The law of love governs both the approach to reading the text and its outcome. Jacobs applies this to the reading of texts other than scripture: 'The universal applicability

---

9. Quoted in Alan Jacobs, *A Theology of Reading: The Hermeneutics of Love* (Boulder, CO: Westview Press, 2001), p. 12.
10. Jeffrey, *People of the Book*, pp. 77-79, including the attribution of Paul's quotations.

of Jesus' twofold commandment makes Augustine's charitable imperative just as relevant to the interpretation of epic poems or national constitutions as it is to the reading of Holy Scripture.'[11] What he is arguing for is that we treat books and authors as neighbours so that, in the way that trusting a loving friend's guidance can lead to understanding, trusting a text and its author can also teach us to see new, previously missed, aspects of the world. Nevertheless, how trustworthy is a neighbourly text? Jacobs reminds us that Kierkegaard pointed out that a neighbour is what philosophers would call the other[12] and this otherness, this difference between neighbour and self, needs to be preserved, both for the successful transmission of ideas and for keeping harmony among different people. As Jacobs says, 'I am to love my neighbour *as* myself, but this is a challenge precisely because the neighbour is *not* myself.'[13]

Since the middle years of the twentieth century, the otherness of the text has again become an important consideration in literary appreciation within several schools of literary criticism under the umbrella of formalism. These focus on form and style, and, of them all, the best known is probably New Criticism. This relies on the otherness of texts and depends on the supposition that, because a text has its own integrity as an artefact which is other than both its creator and its reader, it has something distinctive to say. New Criticism holds the text in high esteem, elevating it to the order of secular scripture as an authoritative entity in its own right. It was, said Jeffrey, 'a distinguished "other"', appreciation of which must be conducted in a 'disinterested manner'.[14] Of course, this disinterestedness is easily compromised and has become a matter of dispute primarily on the basis that it is predicated on a naïve belief in the power of mere signs on a page to communicate meaning. We need not venture too deeply into this literary debate, other than to note, its principal claim that the text is primary. It has priority over its author. The value of a text can outweigh both the reputation and intention of its author. This becomes significant in instances where an author expresses dubious or offensive political or ethical views outside beautiful and affirming texts. The author's personal views need not compromise the value of

---

11. Jacobs, *A Theology of Reading*, p. 11.
12. Ibid., p. 13.
13. Ibid., p. 14.
14. Jeffrey, *People of the Book*, pp. 92-93.

the text. Within a different artistic discipline, in the notorious case of Eric Gill, whose sculptures adorn the exterior walls of the BBC, campaigners seek their removal because it has been shown since Gill's death that he used his eccentricity to cover abusive behaviour towards minors. The debate about whether artists who behave disreputably should be cancelled goes on. To my mind, a reading group I have recently joined pays too much attention to the author of the text we have read at the cost of a proper critique of the text itself. Perhaps, I am discovering that, all along, I have been a New Critic. The relationship of artists to their art, however, is not a new issue. According to the Babylonian Talmud, Tractate 15b, Rabbi Meir was challenged because he continued to consult a former teacher who had lost faith and had become a heretic. The rabbi's response was that he eats 'the inside of the pomegranate, and then I throw away the rind'.[15] This is a principle underpinning my use of literature in forging theology and nurturing spirituality. I accept that there is a strong argument that the behaviour and expressed views of artists can compromise their art but New Criticism offers a convincing counterargument, that the art stands alone and is greater than the artist. If the integrity of a text can be upheld independently of the author, then we preserve its otherness. On this basis, literature from the pens of pagan, irreligious and atheistic authors can contribute to our spiritual selves. Or, to use Jeffrey's imagery, Christian readers can take precious gold from literary Egyptians.[16]

Jacobs's theology of reading seems to argue for an appreciation of literature that is liberal in its techniques, restricted to neither one literary theory nor another. He encourages the practice of charitable reading, the main features of which I shall now discuss.

* * *

As someone who researches literature as an academic, who uses literature in ministry and who reads for relaxation, I am in the curious position of being one who reads for work and pleasure. At various points in my life, I might have read George Eliot's *Adam Bede* when writing for scholars interested in how fiction portrayed Methodism, when preparing for a church book club and when wanting to enjoy a piece of fine writing on a beach holiday (yes, beach holidays are great opportunities for classic reads!). For me, each experience of

---

15. *Times Literary Supplement*, Letters to the Editor, 13 October 2023, p. 6.
16. Jeffrey, *People of the Book*, p. 96.

Reading Charitably

reading the novel was different. My reason for reading, whether for a purpose or only for enjoyment, altered the experience. Why should that be? Why would the reason for reading change the experience? Why should it matter why we are reading? It certainly mattered to Augustine who, in a cautionary note, drew a distinction between *uti* and *frui*, use and enjoyment. He bemoaned the paucity of his education because no one had taught him how to reflect on his reading in a way that would be useful to him. In *Confessions* book one, chapter thirteen he wrote of being encouraged by his teachers to enjoy the *Aeneid*, by which he meant that he was forced to learn about Aeneas's wanderings and to weep for Dido who killed herself for the sake of love. This might seem to be a strange description of what it is to enjoy literature, but there it is. Sometimes one does weep over a novel one enjoys. What disappointed Augustine was that he had not been taught how to put the enjoyment of reading to good use. Reading Aeneas's wanderings had not taught him that he, too, was a wandering, lost soul and reading of Dido's death had not alerted him to the fact that he, too, was 'dying far away' from God. He read and enjoyed it, but he felt that what he read and enjoyed did not teach him much about himself.

Reading merely for enjoyment, Augustine suggests, borders on idolatry. It is a form of book worship. He wants literature to be put to good use, and not merely enjoyed, because using it is for the betterment of our souls and human society. The pleasure of reading, in Augustine's opinion, should lead to lessons learnt. Here, in *De doctrina Christiana*, he writes:

> Some things are to be enjoyed, others to be used, and there are others which are to be enjoyed and used. Those things which are to be enjoyed make us blessed. Those things which are to be used help and, as it were, sustain us as we move toward blessedness in order that we may gain and cling to those things which make us blessed. If we who enjoy and use things, being placed in the middle of things of both kinds, wish to enjoy those things which should be used, our course will be impeded and sometimes deflected, so that we are retarded in obtaining those things which are to be enjoyed, or even prevented altogether, shackled by an inferior love.[17]

---

17. Quoted in Jacobs, *A Theology of Reading*, p. 18.

This is not a disavowal of enjoyment in itself. However, it is to say that, for Augustine, enjoyment should have an edifying purpose. What matters to Augustine is attention to God, not to the book. Jacobs crystalised Augustine's thinking as, 'If attention to God does not *precede* and *envelop* our observations of the world, then these observations are simply idolatrous', where 'the world' includes the books we read.[18] For me, this means that when I read a novel, whether simply for enjoyment or for work, I can read interrogatively, asking the text I am reading an assortment of questions. These might include: What does this novel tell me about God? What are you, the author and your text, trying to teach me about myself and my world? How can what I learn from you improve me? How are you leading me towards the blessedness of which Augustine speaks? Where do I find God in your words and on your pages?

We gain most spiritually from our reading when we read charitably, and this involves four actions the reader should take: to open one's mind; to be aware of presuppositions; to give full attention; and to humble oneself before the text. The first step is to approach the text as if coming to a friend. This entails what Jacobs calls being charitable to the text by being attentive to its intention and by taking account of the spiritual direction towards which it is inclined.[19] Despite Augustine's fear of the corrupting influence of reading only for enjoyment, it is apparent that both pleasure and curiosity are healthy desires if they are bounded by what Augustine called 'rightly ordered love'.[20] In his theology of reading, Jacobs refers to W.H. Auden's comment that, in the way that no one would deny that food and sex can be good in themselves but that an unrestrained pursuit of either is far from good, intellectual curiosity is a similar desire: good in itself, but capable of unhealthy excess. Clearly, pleasure can be derived from purposeful study and, conversely, enjoyment of an interest often leads to study. Which researcher would want to research a subject in which he or she is not interested, and who would not be disappointed if pleasure did not result from learning?

Augustine, nevertheless, argued that reading solely for pleasure is not sinful, unless we pay so much attention to the pleasure of reading that it disrupts the equilibrium of our lives:

---

18. Ibid., p. 21.
19. Ibid., p. 22.
20. Ibid.

> The kind of pleasure we take in a well-crafted work of literary art is very like the pleasure we take in a well-cooked meal, in that it was given to us by another person. ... It is not always appropriate, it is not always charitable, to take that which is offered to us in a spirit of pleasure and recreation and use it according to a rigid criterion of studious application.[21]

Fine dining risks leading to gluttony, but, in itself, it is not sinful. Fine dining can be enjoyed in itself without culinary analysis of technique and critique of presentation. In our age of plenty, fine dining poses greater risks than bibliophilia. Gluttony risks obesity which I am sure is a greater threat to the wellbeing of a society than book worship, although on rare occasions this has led to the theft of rare books from libraries. As a reader using secular literature to fund my spirituality, I am, therefore, much less concerned about literary idolatry than Augustine was. We can read novels for pleasure and for self-improvement, because good reading requires discerning judgement.

The German polymath, Johann Goethe wrote a letter to a friend in which he identified three types of reader: 'one who enjoys without judgement; a third who judges without enjoyment; and one between them who judges as he enjoys and enjoys as he judges. This latter kind really reproduces the work of art anew.'[22] This third type of reader who both enjoys and judges is the reader who reads as a form of spirituality, reading as if for life. This reader achieves the proper balance between enjoyment and use.

The second action required in charitable reading is that the reader should notice the assumptions we bring to the text when we read. During the long year of 2020 – stretching from the worldwide rollout of lockdowns which began in January 2020 to the gradual release of anti-pandemic measures in the late spring of 2021 – greeting strangers when exercising outdoors was one of the unexpected bonuses of that testing time. On several occasions a cheerful greeting might expand into a short conversation perhaps bemoaning the cost to our way of life caused by the virus or expressing longing for better times ahead. Whatever was said in the conversation, and however long or short the conversation was, all those conversations began often cautiously, but

---

21. Cited in ibid., p. 24.
22. Cited in ibid.

with the assumption that the person just met will cause us no harm and may have something intelligible to say. Of course, that assumption may not last for long. We might spot a gun in his hand and back off. Or we might realise that our interlocutor is incoherent and has nothing sensible to say. We might persist with attempts to understand the person with whom we are talking but there will inevitably come a time when we reluctantly abandon what the philosopher Donald Davidson called the 'principle of charity' and the assumption with which we began the conversation.[23] Davidson observes that we do not choose to be charitable; what happens is that we choose to talk to someone and, simply by making that choice, we have assumed a charitable disposition towards that person.

The same principle applies when I pick up a book. I do not expect it to harm me; I do not expect it to be nonsensical; I do not expect it to peddle fake news or untruths. On the contrary, I expect the book to engage with me in a way that will be instructive. I open the book's pages, after examining its cover, blurb, contents and other introductory material, and begin reading with the assumption that it will have something intelligible to say. I shall only abandon this principle of charity towards both the text and the author with great reluctance. There are some readers, indeed, who, as a matter of principle, will never abandon a book. I am not one of these, although there was a time in my younger days when I was very slow to give up on a book. I am a little less patient now. Nevertheless, my assumption always is that the book I have chosen to read has something to say to me.

This almost-involuntary assumption is controlled by our sense of discernment. To understand how this works, allow me to refer to St Basil the Great, the fourth-century bishop of Caesarea, who insisted that almost every pagan author of repute pursued wisdom and virtue. For this reason, he encouraged Christians to read pagan works. They were to approach the text charitably, with the assumption that they would benefit from their engagement with it. However, he advised them to practise discernment. He said that, like bees, who drink the nectar and are nourished by it without taking the entire flower, Christian readers of pagan literature should learn to recognise the presence of wisdom and virtue in the text, while stopping their ears to anything in the text that is not true, good or wise. Even seriously wrong-headed books can thus give nourishment.

---

23. Cited in ibid., p. 31.

Third, readers need to give their full attention to the text because this allows the best opportunity to discern all that the book can offer. Jacobs wrote that 'we owe a debt of loving and constant attentiveness (of faithfulness) to all the books we read – whether they be friends, foes or neighbors'.[24] Thus we place ourselves on 'ground over which variations can be elaborated and developed'. We can play our own variations on the author's themes. These variations are the ideas inferred even from unsympathetic texts by which we can learn more about ourselves. Full attentiveness here means being open to all and any truths within the text, refusing to sacrifice attention to one truth at the expense of another. In the case of the Christian reader, this means not giving priority to an avowedly Christian truth in order to ignore or devalue a wise or virtuous insight from a non-Christian tradition. This might be a hard lesson to learn, and for some difficult to do, but it is the only way our understanding of God deepens and widens. We are to give our attention to what we see and hear of God within the text, however, not to the text itself, for fear of idolising the book. Thus, one reads one's neighbour charitably – whether friend or foe – in order to turn the same full and critical attention on oneself.[25] This provides life-giving self-knowledge.

Take James Robertson's *The Testament of Gideon Mack* for an example of turning critical attention on oneself. This novel concerns a Church of Scotland minister who has disappeared without trace on a Scottish mountain, leaving behind a neatly handwritten manuscript testifying to a lifetime of unbelief and a series of recent encounters seemingly with the supernatural. The first section of the novel comprises a conversation between a journalist, Harry Caithness, and a publisher friend in Edinburgh, Patrick Walker, as they plan to publish the testament which constitutes the body of the novel. An epilogue gives Caithness and Walker an opportunity to reflect on the journal, and includes records of some interviews with some of the other characters involved. These reveal a range of opinion about Gideon and what happened to him.

The son of a church minister, Gideon Mack, has never believed in God and yet he has followed his domineering father into the family profession and tried to be a conscientious pastor to the people of Monimaskit. He remarks that it would be foolish to think that he

---

24. Ibid., p. 67.
25. Ibid., p. 119.

was unique among ministers; he was but one of many 'holy wobblers and switherers making up their numbers'.[26] 'In this life', he says, 'I have lived behind a mask, adapting my disguise as circumstances required. For nearly forty years I have let the world assume that I believed in God when I did not.'[27] Neither the tragic death of his wife, Jenny, in a road accident nor his supposedly consolatory seduction of his best friend's wife, Elsie, trouble him much in terms of religious belief, because the belief was not there to be troubled. His role as a minister in Monimaskit was to be what Jenny had called 'a kind of social worker with an extra qualification in rhetoric'.[28]

All this equilibrium, although it is a compromise, is upset when, while running in the woods, Gideon comes across an eight-feet-tall standing stone in a woodland clearing where none had stood before. Later, while attempting to save a friend's dog, he falls into Black Jaws, a gorge which has claimed many lives before. He is missing for three days in Black Jaws and all assume he has perished but, unexpectedly, he emerges from waters further downstream wearing someone else's shoes. Like the biblical Jacob, he now has a pronounced limp. One leg is an inch shorter than the other, and the femur has been fused as if it had contracted. Gideon's explanation for these mysterious facts is that he had met the Devil while in Black Jaws. There the Devil saved his life and healed his broken leg. The Devil stole his good walking boots and swapped them for his tattered trainers.

Prior to these events, Gideon had struck up a friendship with Catherine Craigie, an eccentric villager housebound by increasingly poor health, for the alleviation of which she smoked cannabis. Congregation members disapproved of this friendship, but the minister and the pagan shared much common ground. When he conducts her funeral after his experience in Black Jaws, he scandalises many of his parishioners by including the non-Christian elements in the rite which Catherine had requested. During the wake, Gideon used the occasion to testify to the mixed-up nature of his belief. He says, 'Catherine didn't believe in ghosts or fairies or God. Neither did I until two weeks ago. No, I do not believe in God. I did not believe there was any life but this one, any world but this world. But in this I

---

26. James Robertson, *The Testament of Gideon Mack* (London: Penguin, 2006), p. 37.
27. Ibid.
28. Ibid., p. 120.

was wrong. I believe now that there is another world beyond ours, a world beyond death, the strangeness and wonderfulness of which we can only guess at.'[29]

His experience in Black Jaws taught him that there is more to life than meets the eye. He has encountered the supernatural and it has disturbed the assumptions he had lived under for over 40 years. Is he mad as some of his parishioners think? Is there madness in religion and religion in madness? Catherine Craigie had regarded herself as agnostic: 'I am only concerned with what we know, what we *can* know.'[30] This is the novel's concern, too. The questions the book poses are: what can Gideon Mack know about God? Does he merely imagine the standing stone whose existence he cannot prove? What really happened in those three days lost in Black Jaws? Is his account of meeting the Devil credible? What other explanation might there be? Most importantly, what impact do his other-worldly experiences have on the nature of belief for him?

These questions are fascinating in the context of the book, but they become vital questions when they are turned on the reader. I found reading *The Testament of Gideon Mack* a challenging experience from start to finish, not because it was a difficult read – in fact, it is so well-written it is a pleasure to read – but because the question the novel asked about Gideon's life turned on me as a Christian believer and minister. A book reads me as much as I read the book. *The Testament of Gideon Mack* challenges me to think about the scope, depth and nature of my belief, to ask what the basics of my faith are. What use do I have in my own belief system for Christian mythology and supernatural beings? I, too, am a minister exercising a post-Enlightenment faith in an enlightened but disenchanted world, believing in a non-interventionist God, wondering how to use Christian mythology without leading others to assume that it is appropriate to take the myths at face value literally, and recognising integrity in the syncretism as espoused by Catherine.

These provocative and illuminating questions arise from a charitable approach to reading whose fourth characteristic is a need for us to humble ourselves before the text as an act of reverence for literature. We must almost deny ourselves before it. The call narrative of the Hebrew prophet Ezekiel ends with a scroll covered front and

---

29. Ibid., p. 340.
30. Ibid., p. 182.

back with words of lamentation, mourning and woe being handed to the prophet with an invitation, 'Mortal, eat this scroll which I give you and fill your stomach with it' (Ezekiel 3:3). When Ezekiel eats the scroll, he is surprised that it is as sweet as honey, not as dry as parchment. The psalmist, too, as well as describing the laws of God as more desirable than even the purest gold, says they taste sweeter than honey (Psalm 19:10). The implication of this Hebrew thinking is that observance of the divine laws has become so second nature to the psalmist that it is as if he has ingested them into his whole being. This seems to have led to a medieval Jewish practice on the Feast of Shavuot, which celebrates the gift of the Torah to the Hebrews, whereby a teacher would show a boy about to be initiated into the faith a slate on which the Hebrew alphabet, a passage from the scriptures and the words, 'May the Torah be your occupation', had been written in chalk. The slate was then covered in honey and the boy instructed to lick the slate clean. In this way the boy ingested the holy words and it became not only his occupation, but part of his being. We know of similar practices in other traditions: Petrarch kissing his copy of Virgil before opening it, Erasmus kissing his copy of Cicero before opening that, and Machiavelli donning his best clothes to read his favourite authors.[31] Dressing to read, rather than for dinner! Presumably, no reading in bed for Machiavelli! That would be too irreverent. The notion of eating or consuming texts also exists in the English literary tradition. In a strange Old English poem, *Solomon and Saturn I*, a dialogue about the Lord's Prayer between the king and a biblical scholar begins with Saturn describing how he has 'tasted the books of all the islands' as he has searched for truth. Having mastered Libyan and Greek science, as well as the history of the Indian Empire, he now longs, with intense hunger, to be overwhelmed by the Lord's Prayer. In the same era, monks used the metaphor of rumination, chewing and digesting food, to describe their meditative technique of reading scripture. A monk would repeat lines of scripture over and over again, feeling them in his mouth and hearing them in his ears, until they became part of him. In this context, we might remember, too, Cranmer's Collect for Bible Sunday which prays that we might "read, mark, learn and inwardly digest" all holy scriptures. The literary commentator, Irina Dumitrescu, observed that we continue

---

31. Fischer, *A History of Reading*, p. 218.

to use this idea of eating text when we use the term 'chewing the cud' to describe meditating over something.[32]

These may be extreme expressions of reverence for the word, yet they relate to some aspects of a more common approach to reading. The quite disgusting notion of licking books and ingesting the word is less repugnant if we think of it as ruminating upon the text in concentrated reading and meditation, in such a focussed manner that its full flavour is released and its full meaning sounded. Ritualised consumption or ingestion of a revered text is similar to learning by heart, by which we allow the import of the text to influence every aspect of our being, letting it sink into our bones. According to Jacobs, this is a form of self-loss, or self-emptying before the text. We immerse and lose ourselves in what we read, a facet of reading we shall explore further in Chapter Four. Jacobs refers to an incident in Iris Murdoch's novel *The Unicorn*, where her character Max is about to drown. Max had always known about death on an intellectual level, but now that he faces its immanent reality, he realises that the death of self can be an act of love. To love was 'to look and look until one exists no more' because loving another is self-denying. The ultimate death of self that results from absolute love for another makes the world 'the object of perfect love'.[33]

In what sense do readers immerse and lose themselves in books? In what sense do authors humble themselves before readers on the publication of their books? To what extent is the publication of a book an act of authorial self-submission? How does this shared self-immolation before the text work, with regard to spirituality?

St Luke recounts Jesus's parable of the prodigal son so effectively that we cannot resist placing ourselves in the narrative. Usually called the parable of the prodigal son because its companion parables in chapter fifteen are those of the lost coin and the lost sheep, as a parable describing the economy of the kingdom of God it could equally well be titled the parable of the waiting father. Or, indeed, given the challenging way it ends it could be called the parable of the elder brother. What you choose to call it is significant, for it may indicate with which character you most readily identify. Are you the lost son who has realised he must find his way back to his father and

---

32. Irina Dumitrescu, 'Eating Their Words', *Times Literary Supplement*, 30 September 2022, p. 27.
33. Iris Murdoch, *The Unicorn* (London: Chatto & Windus, 1963), p. 198.

plead for admission? Or are you the lost son who has not yet come to this realisation and needs to hear that your father is looking out for you, waiting for you to return and will run out to bring you home once he has you in his sightline? Or are you the elder brother who never even thought of leaving home and now resents the undeserved welcome lavished on the wastrel who has now returned? The parable 'works' when readers find their place in the narrative and are thus challenged either not to resent the forgiveness shown to another who repents, or to turn back to God from whom they have either strayed or intentionally withdrawn. Finding your place in the parable requires you to let go of any reservations you have about yourself and allow yourself to fall into, and become lost in, the story.

Simon Mawer's *The Fall* (2003) is one novel I lost myself in. When a novelist with a known interest in religious themes – previous novels included *The Bitter Cross* set during the Reformation and *The Gospel of Judas* which fictionalises the story of the discovery of the eponymous document – publishes a book called *The Fall* using the definite article, Christian and Jewish readers will assume the title refers to the primal myth of Adam and Eve, whose fall from grace banished humankind from paradise. In fact, Simon Mawer's *The Fall* tells of several falls – from innocence, from virginity, from the North Face of the Eiger and from a suicidally dangerous unprotected climb across a vertical rock slab in Snowdonia – none of which is inevitable. Nor can anyone fully recover from the after effects of any of these falls. The novel shows how puny humanity is when set against the forces of nature, whether the forces one is up against are sexual drives or the elements encountered on the mountainside.

The novel begins one spring morning in the 1980s as one of a group of walkers points out a solitary middle-aged man, without helmet or rope, crawling along an almost sheer rock face seventy feet above them. To their horror they see him fall to his death. News that this is Jim Matthewson one of the great climbers of the modern era brings an old boyhood friend, Rob Dewar, to Wales for the funeral. He gives the eulogy. Another friend Dominic Lewis 'mumbled a poem about Icarus falling from the sky. Auden, I suppose'.[34] Many of you will recognise this as Auden's 'Musée des Beaux Arts' which we shall discuss in a later chapter. In contrast with the walkers who had been transfixed by Jim's climb and fall, the poem describes the disinterest

---

34. Simon Mawer, *The Fall* (London: Little, Brown, 2003), p. 28.

of sailors and a ploughman as Icarus falls and plunges into the waves from which he will not emerge. They all calmly carry on with their lives as if Icarus had not fallen.

Life goes on for Mawer's characters, too, despite the human susceptibility to falling. Most of the novel looks back from Jim's unproven suicide in the 1980s to the years of Jim and Rob's earlier climbing career, which had begun in the early 1960s, and further back still to uncover the story of their parents' complex relationships in and around wartime.

There is a strong sexual undercurrent to Jim and Rob's friendship when young: a girl called Bethan removes her clothes to satisfy their curiosity about the anatomy of the female body – although she is careful not to allow them to touch because that would be 'dirty'. Later, the boys' first climb together ends awkwardly, when, after Jim has coaxed Rob to scramble up a quarry face, the security guard chases them off but abducts Jim and takes him to the security hut where Jim seems to allow himself to be abused. Later, when Rob is sixteen, Jim's mother, Caroline, invites him to London, but, when Rob arrives, he discovers Jim is not at home as he expected. The invitation seems to have been a ploy to give Caroline the opportunity to seduce him. Having already fallen from innocence, he now falls from virginity.

These sexual experiences have counterparts in the stories of the previous generation. In one glorious climbing expedition together in the Welsh mountains, Diana and Guy, Rob's mother and Jim's father, abandon themselves to a 'last fling' before Diana leaves to take up wartime nursing duties. She warns Guy to be careful:

> but then it was too late to do anything about it, for they were falling. She cried out with the shock of it, the feeling of release and the thrill of fear. It would stop, she knew that – a fall must always come to a stop eventually – but for the moment she didn't care: there was just the sensation of falling, and the shock, and Guy clinging to her.[35]

On this weekend they had 'fallen in love, made love, ascended four rock climbs, had breakfast, lunch and supper, argued, shouted, laughed and cried'.[36] This last throw of the dice before parting is described throughout as 'falling'.

---

35. Ibid., p. 166.
36. Ibid., p. 169.

Similar sexual experiences occur in the later generation's adult lives: in the 1960s, Jim, Rob and Ruth go to the Alps where, before an attempt on the North Face of the Eiger, Ruth engages with both young men in a threesome. Breakfast the next morning was eaten in silence: 'It was the silence after the fall.'[37]

The more serious falls are those from rockfaces: Jim's apparently suicidal fall in the Prologue, his father Guy's fatal fall in the Himalayas and, most importantly, Rob's near-fatal fall from the North Face of the Eiger, an account of which occupies about one eighth of the novel. Chapter nineteen immersed me in an account of climbing the Eiger, which is but one of several such accounts in the novel. They are totally engrossing in their detail and suspense, even for non-climbers like me. The climbers, despite their strength and agility, are puny and fragile when pitted against the elements. Their cries for help seem hopeless, almost futile: 'Our shouts were pulverised by the wind, torn apart, battered and shredded into mere fragments of sound';[38] and, as he lay waiting for rescue, 'I shivered and hunched and no longer thought much about anything, neither death nor survival, neither hope nor despair … some abstract part of me knew that this was my life ebbing away.'[39] Their puny insignificance in contrast with the magnificence of the mountains is a form of self-loss. They have to submit themselves to the rock to master it.

There is an additional fall in the novel – mine when I let myself go into the narrative of the book, when I immerse myself into the context of the story and the novel's fictional world, and where I can begin to make sense of the actual world I live in, knowing both myself and God better than I previously did. This is possibly the most important fall in the novel, for it is this letting go which funds spirituality when I read. It might occur suddenly when an opening sentence pulls me in, as suddenly as a leap from an aeroplane for a skydive, which I am told is more like a rolling fall from the door than a jump. An outstanding example of this immediate fall occurred when I read the first paragraphs of the late Iain Banks's *Whit* (1995). They recounted an incident in which the novel's protagonist, at five years of age, resuscitated a dead fox by burying her nose in its fur, to the disgust of her older brother who had just found it in a hedgerow. This extraordinary behaviour rapidly engaged me in the

---

37. Ibid., p. 298.
38. Ibid., p. 328.
39. Ibid., p. 340.

fictional world of *Whit*, a satire on the role of religious faith in modern society centred on a mysterious Scottish cult. Banks, of course, had a remarkable gift for writing attention-grabbing openings. Few can be more attention-grabbing than the opening sentence of *The Crow Road* (1992): 'It was the day my grandmother exploded.' After such an opener, how can one not surrender to the text?

On other occasions, the reader's fall into a novel may be as gentle and cautious as my gradual inching into a river for a cold-water swim. Whether immediate or gradual, my fall into the text I am reading is the way friendships are formed. Friendships develop only when two people permit themselves to trust the other person sufficiently to let go of all the masks and safety nets they might use to protect themselves. After all, you cannot love another unless you expose yourself to the risk of not being loved, and you cannot fully engage with a text unless you immerse yourself in it. Of course, there are risks associated with this – and this is perhaps why some so-called wise, but actually mistaken, men of old cautioned against reading novels – but the conclusion I have reached from a lifetime of reading is that, in contrast with any puritanical tendency towards distrust of novels, the risks are worthwhile for I soon find that they are friends. Moreover, I can learn from them about myself and about God.

4

Circling the Text

Aristotle described friendship as a slow ripening fruit; and some recent studies in the University of Kansas have shown that it takes over two hundred hours for strangers to become good friends. One reason for this is that there is always some degree of suspicion or distrust towards strangers on first meeting, before we are comfortable enough to be prepared to take the risk of opening our hearts and hands to the other. Friendship relies on taking the risk that a friend may, in time, hurt you. Friendship relies on openness to the other, to the exposure to the risk of hurt and to the potential of love. The good friend is not an object of adulation but an equal partner in risk and love. Similarly, when books are your friends, maintaining a healthy friendship matters.

Bibliophilia, the love of books, can descend into a syndrome and a health disorder. In my college days, I recall a fellow student who bought books almost on a daily basis and often proudly displayed his overflowing book shelves to visitors, but he showed few signs of having read any of them. He was no more than a book collector – and what use are books when on the shelves, other than for decoration? Loving the book for itself is a form of idolatry, the danger of which is most acute when the book in question is the Christian Bible. Processed into church to mark the beginning of an act of worship, held aloft as the Gospel is read in church, and grasped when giving an oath in court, the Bible is often used as an object to be revered simply for what it is. However, as Daniel Coleman points out, even for St Augustine, for whom the Scriptures were the holiest of writings, the

Bible 'is a vehicle for the journey rather than its destination'.[1] The church in which I learnt my faith was rather biblio-centric. Sunday school taught the Bible's stories and all our lessons were based on Bible reading. Church services were mostly preaching services with an expectation that sermons were usually expository and were not expected to employ biblical criticism that risked disturbing what many valued as 'simple faith'. My understanding of church, its liturgy, teaching and purpose, has certainly broadened out since then. I think of the Bible differently now and I read it differently; but I still love it. I would most certainly want it with me on any desert island to which BBC Radio 4 might send me as a castaway. I love it, though, not for itself, but as a guide to lead me on the way to elsewhere, out of myself and closer to God, out of preoccupation with my own concerns to a more charitable disposition towards others. It stands beside me pointing the way, as well as before me urging me to step forward. This healthy impetus is lost if ever I love the book, Good Book though it is, for itself alone. I would then have fallen into the error of bibliolatry.

Thankfully, the trend in contemporary society is a move away from literary idolatry. Books are revered less than other media. Books ask you to make time for them and to take time with them. Most other media encourage the opposite. Other media offer more instant gratification: save time, watch a two-hour film of a book rather than spend a few days with the book itself. We are constantly being distracted: as I write this paragraph messages appear on my screen alerting me to the arrival of emails. How irritating! As I drive through the streets of outer London, billboards try to take my eyes from the road ahead and, as I travel on the underground, the thoroughfares, the platforms and the trains are plastered with advertisements seeking to grab my attention – even if just for a moment. These try to play on my restlessness and discontent; they try to rush me on to try something new that will enhance my life in a trice. The exercise machines in the local gym stand in front of giant television screens lest I become bored with exercise, and conversation with friends in a pub is hampered by all-round television sets vying for attention. Any invitation to read a novel is, therefore, counter-cultural. The reader must slow down and find quiet time. Reading novels is best done slowly and meditatively, neither hastily nor with a deadline for completion. Reading is not a race to completion. Reading a novel requires more

---

1. Coleman, *In Bed with the Word*, p. 25.

effort than watching the film of a book; it is more active than passive. Moreover, it exercises the reader's imagination: neither the scenes nor the characters are before our eyes on screen as they would be if we were watching a film. The reader must hear any dialogue through the eyes from the words on the page, not through the ears. This requires work, which, as Coleman says, 'runs in the opposite direction from the one in which Western commodity culture is running'.[2]

The effect on our spirituality of this necessary slowing down in order to read fiction is twofold. First, it makes us more contemplative. The old adage from the early years of television was that the pictures were better on the radio, and the adage has stuck, even after the advent of television's full colour pictures, high-definition screens and three-dimensional films. This is an interesting thought because radio can be thought of as being sensorily sparse: it uses nothing other than sound to communicate a world that elsewhere uses all the senses to communicate with us. Books are similarly sensorily limited. When we are reading, we have to put ourselves to the tasks of scanning the pages with our eyes, recognising marks on the pages that carry meaning and interpreting those meanings. This requires us to deploy imagination, our most useful tool when taking in the world around us. We cannot see, smell, touch, taste or hear the world of the book; all we can do is read words that are one step removed from the world they convey. The effort of reading makes us slow down and we learn to appreciate 'the pleasures of reflection, the relief of not being restless and of having time to follow a complete thought that has not been reduced to a soundbite or an advertiser's slogan'.[3] We learn the art of silence, slowness, reflection and internally generated imagination – the art of contemplation.

The second effect on our spirituality of taking time for reading is that it awakens our critical awareness. Because it requires active interpretation of the text rather than passive receptivity to what the mass media want to tell us, it produces what Coleman calls 'critically alert' readers rather than 'naively accepting' readers.[4] These are less likely to be duped by whichever worldly power wants to ply its wares and philosophies on unsuspecting consumers and citizens.

---

2. Ibid., p. 26.
3. Ibid., p. 31.
4. Ibid., p. 32.

We should, therefore, be suspicious of what we read. Paul Ricoeur (1913-2005) was a philosopher whose theory of the interpretation of texts introduced the notion of a hermeneutics of suspicion. This stands as an opposite pole to the hermeneutic of affirmation, which he also called the hermeneutic of faith. This hermeneutic of faith is the assumption that the process of reading and interpretation uncovers and takes in the intended meaning already present within the text. For this to happen the text must be revered, appreciated and sympathetically analysed for its truth and beauty. On its own, this is inadequate, because, so Ricoeur argued, texts are not innocent and pure, and they cannot be fully aware of the implications of, or the motivations for, their contents. For meaningful interpretation, readers need to discover what lies behind and within a text's lack of self-awareness. To achieve this, readers must strip away any illusions texts have about themselves and any disguises they might be wearing. During the pandemic we might have said that masks should be removed when we read.

Ricoeur was careful to say that readers must not choose between the hermeneutics of suspicion or faith when reading, but that both faith in the text and suspicion of the text should be held in tension. I, for instance, read the parable of the prodigal son trusting that it carries something of God which I shall find enlightening and affirming but, to gain most from the story, I should also read it suspecting that it has more to say than its author thinks it has. I should also be open to the possibility that it might mislead me.

Coleman contends that the tension between these two poles can be seen in the pendulum swings of literary criticism in the two halves of the twentieth century. In the first half, in what was known as New Criticism, students were taught to appreciate the subtlety and ingenuity of literature, venerating the text itself and taking little notice of the context in which these usually white, middle- or upper-class men wrote their works. Since the 1960s, however, literary appreciation has widened out and swung the other way. Critics noted women's perspectives, working-class experiences, the work of black and indigenous authors and the previously closeted voices of gay and lesbian writers coming to the fore. Reading is now seen to have social and political dimensions that had previously been either ignored or suppressed. In such a cornucopia of literature, readers would be remiss if they uncritically admired whatever they were reading. We have, therefore, learnt to examine all texts with suspicion so that we can see how their unspoken assumptions try to shape us and control our thinking.

What I welcome about this development in literary criticism is that it has opened the floodgates for the publication and reading of a greater variety of literature. Working class writers such as Alan Sillitoe, post-colonial writers such as Salman Rushdie, writers from within the LGBTQ+ communities such as Jeanette Winterson, and many more, are now readily available to all of us and their work opens up to us the worlds from which they come. Given the multiplicity of this variety, holding the tension between, on the one hand, reading affirmatively or faithfully and, on the other, more cautious reading with a hermeneutic of suspicion is especially important. One without the other is deficient.

Moreover, Ricoeur's theory gives me permission, should I have ever needed it, to venture outside the camp of the traditional literary canon, the so-called Great Tradition. It teaches me that I cannot treat the Great Tradition with blind trust and faith; I must examine and challenge it. It encourages me to look outside the canon for truth and beauty in full expectation that I shall find them there. Once a reader has become critically aware in this way, the reading of any text has most certainly become a spiritual exercise. As Coleman artfully says in conclusion to his book, 'We will find that even books of sorrow, even books of devastation, along with books of surprise and books of confirmation, can be books that taste sweet as honey.'[5] The scroll with bitter words of lamentation and mourning that Ezekiel was given to eat also tasted sweet as honey.[6]

The Reader charity, which began in the University of Liverpool in 1997 with the purpose of taking serious literature into hard-to-reach and easy-to-ignore communities, teamed up with the university's Centre for Research into Reading, Literature and Society in 2008 to try out a Shared Reading programme. This involved diverse people reading live, aloud and together in groups, with intervals for focussed analysis and personal reflection, led by a trained project worker. Note that this differs from regular book clubs or reading groups, where the membership is more homogenous, where the books are read in advance and where discussion is on the basis of opinion reached in retrospect. Reporting on this research, Philip Davis expressed himself

---

5. Ibid., p. 128.
6. Ezekiel 3:3.

firm in the belief that those who participated were 'more' for having read literature.[7] He remains vague about what this means – increased self-esteem and confidence, mostly, but also better understanding of circumstances, as well as recovery from disillusionment – but it is interesting to note that he may also be implying an element of spirituality in it. He says, '*Reading for Life* is not about religious experience as such, but it is about individual acts of triggered contemplation that for some readers have had to become a replacement for religion in the search for human meaning amidst the deeper, darker strata of inner human reality'.[8] The communities in which Shared Reading was used were often communities where churches are absent or less influential. Those involved in the groups did not have easy access to traditional spiritual resources. Shared Reading stepped into gaps vacated by institutional religion.

I refer to this research programme because it identifies three phases of contemplative reading to travel through as we approach a text. The first of the three phases is Getting In, which, in the programme's methodology, is about getting the story or poem into the room and getting the people in the group to feel it. The next is Staying In, which requires rereading repeatedly and encourages participants to stay with lines, phrases and words so that they become immersed in the text without distraction. The last stage is Break-Through [sic], when the text strikes home.[9] This might take some time but, if the readers stay in the text long enough, something will happen. Davis reports one participant describing this breakthrough of immersion in the book in terms of being like a spiritual figure looking over it all and having some supernatural awareness, and another speaking of the breakthrough being like an epiphany, an 'Aha!' moment of self-recognition in the text. Similarly, I can think of Bible passages that have meant little to me, and puzzled me, but circumstances changed and, after many years of a form of redundancy, they speak to me with deep meaning. Break-Through can be after minutes, or decades.

There is much more that could be said about this research programme, which is so exciting for lovers of literature because it has such improving effects on people's lives. The programme is so much

---

7. Philip Davis, *Reading for Life* (Oxford: Oxford University Press, 2020), p. 19.
8. Ibid., p. 5.
9. Ibid., p. 25.

more than a three-phase pattern of reading, but it is this pattern that informs the spirituality of reading I am considering in this discussion.

My overall impression of this research programme is that suspicion is a significant factor at play when group facilitators use the Getting-In, Staying-In, Break-Through pattern. For instance, in the final chapter of his report, Davis tells of one group he had been working with. It met in a secure psychiatric hospital for those who present a grave danger to themselves or others. Most were there after a prison sentence. The researchers found that individuals in the group set up more defence barriers than previously encountered in any other reading group. Participants seemed so resistant and erected so many protective barriers that the group lacked connection with each other and the texts. Getting In was a slow process lasting several months. Nevertheless, breakthroughs came.

One came when reading 'Along the Road' by Robert Browning Hamilton, the first stanza of which describes a walk with an allegorical figure called Pleasure who 'chattered all the way, / But left me none the wiser / For all she had to say'. In the second stanza, the walk is with Sorrow who is silent throughout, 'But, oh, the things I learned from her / When Sorrow walked with me!'[10] The breakthrough occurred when the group leader, deliberately employing the vocabulary of the poem, asked what 'thing' one might learn from sorrow. After silence, one man said, 'Regret', then, after another long pause, he changed his answer to 'Remorse'. That single word struck home. It was a word most of the group members would avoid. They would be suspicious of the word as one often bandied around in therapy sessions, something they are told they ought to feel. However, now they have found the word for themselves as a result of reading a poem aloud together. All of this, Davis often says in his report, is risky. Facilitators take risks with the texts in the groups. Perhaps the risk overcomes the suspicion and perhaps, if there were no risk involved, there would be no need to be suspicious.

This three-phase pattern can be represented as a circle. Getting In is a process of orbiting around the text to find an entry point; Staying In, as repeated rereading, can be compared to going round and round the text; and the Break-Through comes when the reader breaks out of the circle into its centre.

---

10. Quoted in ibid., p. 268.

That the process can be represented in diagrammatic form as a series of circles should cause no surprise, for, according to the American essayist Ralph Waldo Emerson, everything is circular or cyclical. In an essay published in 1841, entitled 'Circles', Emerson said, 'The life of man is a self-evolving circle, which, from a ring imperceptibly small, rushes on all sides outwards to new and larger circles, and that without end.' At the beginning of the essay, he had said that the eye is the first circle, the horizon it sees is the second and, throughout nature, this circular figure is repeated without end, because, he said, God is a circle whose centre is everywhere and whose circumference is nowhere. In other words, Emerson saw human development as a process of enlargement by which we move outwards from our immature egotistical perception of the world confined entirely to ourselves, through ever expanding circles towards the ineffability of God.[11] For Emerson, literary education was a matter of ever-expanding circles. We can be hemmed in to our current worldview:

> [b]ut if the soul is quick and strong, it bursts over that boundary on all sides, and expands another orbit on the great deep, which also runs up into a high wave, with attempt again to stop and to bind. But the heart refuses to be imprisoned; in its first and narrowest pulses, it already tends outward with a vast force, and to immense and innumerable expansions.'[12]

Emerson's notion here that there is within us a natural and improving tendency to expand outwards through ever-expanding circles, while interesting, is not without difficulties: Is it fair to assume that the next move outwards is inevitably good for the soul and enhances life? Are there times when it would be appropriate to step back or stand still? For these reasons, and to establish a fuller picture of the spirituality of reading, I want to complicate Emerson's image with series of more circles – circles that rise up and circles that drill down.

For the circles that rise up, we turn to a work of classical spirituality, Teresa of Avila's *The Interior Castle*. Teresa was a Spanish Carmelite nun, a mystic who wrote *The Interior Castle* in 1577 as a guide for

---

11. Mark Edmundson, *Why Read?* (New York, NY: Bloomsbury, 2004), p. 30.
12. Quoted in ibid.

spiritual development and prayer. It was inspired by her vision of the soul as a diamond in the shape of a castle containing seven mansions. She interpreted this as a representation of stages on the journey of faith that ends in union with God. In the book she describes the faithful making progress through seven successive interior courts.

In the first court, the soul is in a state of grace but surrounded by sin, while seeking grace through humility. The second mansion describes the practice of prayer where the soul seeks to advance towards God by thinking daily about God. These thoughts evolve into prayer. The third stage describes the exemplary life where the individual develops an aversion of both mortal and venial sin and desires to do charitable work in order to bring glory to God. The fourth stage is a transitional stage in which the individual moves from needing to work hard in order to pray to being a person able to pray naturally because God is active within. Teresa describes this as a 'temple of solitude'. The fifth stage is what she calls 'the prayer of union' where the soul falls asleep to the things of the world and becomes united with God. The next stage is one of betrothal to God where the individual experiences extraordinary mystical phenomena such as visions, raptures and ecstasies mixed with terrible times of suffering, through which, the soul, like a faithful spouse, remains faithful. The final stage is a second heaven where spiritual marriage transforms the soul to such an extent that the individual forgets self, becomes detached from everything temporal, and feels strong and calm because of the constant presence of the Bridegroom. Of course, the imagery of marriage to God, typical of that period in Catholic history, is increasingly problematic in current times. What interests me about Teresa's schema is that the castle is almost always depicted as a circle or helix. Illustrations depict the soul's journey along the seven stages and through the interior castle as a rising circle. Let's hold on to this as an image for the soul's progress towards God.

The other circling associated with reading involves drilling down. As a former English teacher, I, of course, enjoy seeing a child read. I also enjoy watching readers on trains and buses. In summer it is lovely to see readers lolling on the grass with a book. What I enjoy about all these scenes is the absorption and concentration I observe. When readers are fully engrossed in their book, oblivious to all that may be going on around them, they have drilled down into its pages and immersed themselves in the book's world. In so doing, they circle down into themselves, their pasts, their true nature, their joys and their pains.

In short, I am arguing that the act of reading takes readers in at least three directions along paths of concentric circles: the first is an ever-widening one of increased learning and understanding; the second is a rising circle towards God and godliness; and the third is a downward spiral into deeper self-awareness. Thus, says Edmundson, we 'make contact with one's outer-lying circles'.[13] The expansion of one's orbits, he argues, is good for the individual and good for society, so this is inevitably a point of personal growth for the reader.

* * *

To demonstrate how these circles might work for us, I turn to a classic literary text: Thomas Hardy's *Tess of the d'Urbervilles* (1891). A reminder of the plot will inform my later comments about the circles of *Tess*.

This is the story of a pure woman, as the subtitle describes her, and the novel offers what Hardy, in his poem 'In Tenebris II', called 'a full look at the Worst', necessary as a possible 'way to the Better'. Herein lies the creative tension of this novel, which marked the beginning of the end of Hardy's novel writing. Soon after publishing *Tess*, he put down his novelistic pen to focus on poetry, partly in reaction to the novel's critical reception: it provoked an outcry which Hardy regarded as unfair and unnecessary. There would be only one further book, *Jude the Obscure* (1895). *Tess* was, to some extent, a parody of an Evangelical tract, in particular, a parody of the most popular of them, Legh Richmond's *The Dairyman's Daughter* of 1809. In Richmond's tale, the eponymous Betsy is saved by an itinerant preacher, whereas Tess is progressively corrupted and destroyed by her contact with various exponents of Evangelicalism. This is a pastoral novel set several decades before the time of writing which gives Hardy an opportunity to describe a rural way of life at the cusp of the mechanisation of agriculture and a Church of England challenged from within by the Oxford Movement and from without by scientific advances and industrialisation which moved the population into new unchurched urban centres. Most significantly, *Tess* is a tragedy which contrasts sharply with the Christian metanarrative which is essentially what Dante called 'a divine comedy', a tale with a happy ending. The only happy ending in *Tess* is a compromised one: Tess's young sister walks

---

13. Ibid., p. 31.

off in the early morning hand in hand with the man Tess has truly loved as a black flag flies announcing Tess's death.

Tess's story is told in seven phases, beginning with an ominous encounter – a chance meeting between Parson Tringham and John Durbeyfield, a travelling market trader, in which the parson carelessly tells Durbeyfield that he a descendent of the d'Urbervilles, an ancient, monied family who had land holdings as far back as the time of William the Conqueror. Soon after this life-transforming discovery, hardship falls on the family as a result of an accident in which its workhorse, Prince, is killed. Tess blames herself for this loss of the only means of income the family has. The Durbeyfield family learns that a 'relative' lives nearby. John and his wife, Joan, send their sixteen-year-old daughter, Tess, to 'claim kin' in order to alleviate their impoverished condition. While visiting the d'Urbervilles at the Slopes, Tess meets Alec d'Urberville, who arranges for Tess to become the caretaker of his blind mother's poultry. The good fortune of discovering wealthy ancestors and relatives is the cause of Tess's downfall: Alec seduces and rapes Tess in a secluded wood. 'Where was Tess's guardian angel? Where was the providence of her simple faith? Perhaps, like that other god of whom the ironical Tishbite spoke, he was talking, or he was pursuing, or he was on a journey, or he was sleeping and not to be awaked', chapter eleven declaims. She was a maiden no more, as the title of phase two of the novel describes her.

Shamed by the experience and already wishing that she had never been born, Tess returns home, for the greater part of the journey driven by her seducer who cannot at all understand why she is upset. Joan Durbeyfield assumes, at first, that Tess has returned home to be married; but, no, Tess's mother was showing her foolishness. Tess remains and gives birth to a son, whom she names Sorrow, Alec's unwanted child. Tess maintains herself and her son by working as a field worker on nearby farms until Sorrow becomes ill and dies. His dying so young leaves Tess devastated and she makes yet another journey away from home to nearby Talbothays Dairy to become a milkmaid in the employment of a good-natured dairyman, Mr Crick. There she meets and falls in love with a travelling farmer's apprentice, Angel Clare. Despite her love for Angel, her prior experiences lead her to try to resist Angel's entreaties for her hand in marriage. When she can withstand his wishes no longer, she succumbs and they marry. She has found it impossible to tell him what Alec d'Urberville had done to her so, until they marry, Angel has an incomplete understanding of her past. After the wedding, Tess and Angel confess their pasts to each other. Tess, out of love for him, readily forgives Angel for his past indiscretions but, in the fifth phase of the book, 'The Woman Pays', we learn that Angel cannot forgive Tess. He is unable to forgive what conventional society in the 1890s regarded as her sins, even though she has forgiven his. This is a familiar theme in Hardy's work: the misfortune that befalls any characters who are unable to forgive as they have been forgiven renders profoundly Christian the morality that underpins his narratives.

Angel coldly suggests that the couple should separate, with Angel going to Brazil for a year and Tess going back home. Without explaining the circumstances to her parents, Tess agrees and returns to their home. Tess eventually leaves home again to work at Flintcomb-Ash Farm, described as a 'starve-acre place' (chapter 43). The working conditions in the, at times, rain-sodden and, at other times, frozen fields are very harsh. She continues to look for correspondence from Angel, who had implied that he would tell her his whereabouts in Brazil so that she might join him. One Sunday, just a day short of a year since their marriage, Tess made her way to Emminster vicarage, the address to which Angel had said he would send his letters. Nothing awaits her there. However, as she passes a barn on the way back, she hears a preacher whom the locals regard as 'an excellent, fiery, Christian man' (chapter 44). In phase six we meet this preacher and discover he is Alec, now described as 'The Convert' and practising as an evangelical minister, preaching from village to village and attracting large crowds. When Alec sees Tess, he is struck dumb. Very soon he leaves his position to pursue her.

When Alec catches up with Tess, he confirms that he now desists from preaching, states he has lost his religious belief and asks her to marry him. It is, in his view, the honourable thing for him to do and he follows her to Flintcomb, persisting in his request that she marry him. Tess refuses in the strongest terms. Tess is called home because her mother is ill, although on her return she finds that her mother is recovering. However, her father dies suddenly from an unknown ailment and the burden of her family's welfare falls on Tess's shoulders. His death has left the family destitute and homeless after being evicted from their cottage. Because the Durbeyfields have nowhere to go, Tess now knows that she can no longer resist the allure of Alec's money and the comforts it could provide for her family. Furthermore, Alec insists that Angel will never return and has abandoned her – an idea that Tess has already come to believe herself. Thus, Tess and Alec leave for Sandbourne, a fashionable resort on the south coast.

Meanwhile, contrary to Tess's expectations and to Alec's ploy, Angel has returned from Brazil to look for Tess with the intention of using the money he had earned in Brazil to establish his own farm with Tess in England. When Angel finds Tess's family, Joan tells him he is too late: Tess has left for Sandbourne. Despite Joan's advice, Angel follows her and finds her living as an upper-class lady with Alec d'Urberville. Tess asks Angel to leave and never return. Honourably, Angel leaves, resigned to the fact that he had judged Tess too harshly and returned too late.

However, after this meeting with Angel, Tess confronts Alec and accuses him of concealing Angel's return from her. During the argument that follows, in a fit of anger and fury, Tess stabs Alec through the heart with a carving knife, killing him. Immediately, Tess seeks out Angel to tell him what she has done and they flee together. The trail ends for them at the ancient pagan monument of Stonehenge, when the pursuing police catch them, arrest Tess and take her away.

Tess's execution for the murder of Alec is inevitable but, before the hanging, Tess makes Angel promise to marry her sister, Liza Lu, after her death. Angel agrees and the novel ends with him and Liza Lu watching a black flag being raised in the city of Wintoncester as a signal that Tess's death sentence has been fulfilled. Readers are left wondering whether Tess's hanging is 'The Fulfilment' alluded to in the title of the final phase. Angel and Liza Lu, once they have recovered from the sight, join hands and leave together. Thus, the tragic tale of Tess ends and the narrator remarks that: '"Justice" was done, and the President of the Immortals ... had ended his sport with Tess.'

Even if you find this a relentlessly gloomy narrative, what has unfolded in the tale is a novel which has continued to reward me in the 50 years since I first read it. It circles outwards into aspects of human society in its depiction of the agricultural world of the mid-nineteenth century at a time of great change, upwards into facets of God and downwards into the essence of what it is to be human. The polyphony of the novel form allows this wide range because it gives to novels an indeterminate form which allows a creative free exploration of ideas. Let us look more closely at this by considering some of the questions that circle *Tess of the d'Urbervilles*.

First, does Christianity diminish humanity? Hardy saw Christianity as a worldview that diminished humanity, in particular,

Circling the Text

womankind. I am not sure I saw Hardy's empathy with his female characters when I first read the book as a seventeen-year-old pupil but, when I look again at the conversation between Tess and Alec after he has raped her, I see it. Alec has little comprehension of the hurt he has caused. Nor does he understand that he had misled Tess. She admits that her 'eyes had been dazed by [him] for a while' but says that she had not understood his meaning until it was too late. 'That's what every woman says', is his dismissive response. I think I hear Hardy's voice in Tess's rejoinder: 'My God! Did it never strike your mind that what every woman says some women may feel?' (chapter twelve). More generally, Hardy saw Christian doctrine as making people worse than they truly are. We see this in the incident of the baptism and burial of Tess's baby, Sorrow. Fearing that Sorrow would be consigned to hell if he died unbaptised, Tess baptises him herself. When she asks the parson, who had arrived too late to conduct the baptism, to perform a Christian burial the parson is sympathetic but 'the man and the ecclesiastic fought within him'. What he, as a compassionate human being, wanted to do his church would not allow him to do. He reassures Tess about the validity of her baptism of Sorrow, but says he 'must not' bury the child. Tess is reduced to burying her son in what the narrator describes as 'that shabby corner of God's allotment where He lets the nettles grow' (chapter fourteen). In what theology is it right to toy with and demean humanity in this way? Can humankind not hold its head high? After the rape, Tess feels that she has been made to break a social law and she describes herself as 'a figure of Guilt intruding into the haunts of Innocence' (chapter thirteen). We cannot avoid seeing that, regardless of how she is treated, Tess is nothing other than a pure woman and is far from deserving of maltreatment or ill fortune. She is, as Hardy says, like a bird caught in a springe. The narrator considers the possibility that Tess's violation may have been a form of punishment, not in retribution of any action of hers, but for the misdeeds of her male ancestors. Even so, the narrator opines that this is unfair: 'To visit the sins of the fathers upon the children may be a morality good enough for divinities [but] it is scorned by average human nature.' Hardy's discussion of the nature of humanity through this novel provokes us to seek a form of Christianity that does not belittle humankind.

The apparent weighting of the scales against Hardy's characters as if to ensure their defeat and their helpless inability to swing the balance back in their favour has frustrated many of his readers. Unexpected accidents and unfortunate coincidences occur regularly in his tragic novels and often in his other literature. It is as if he purposefully sets chance and circumstance against any prospect of human happiness. Tess's misplaced letter is a fine example. Tess tries to avoid calamity by writing a four-page confessional to Angel informing him of her previous liaison with Alec. Two or three nights before she is due to marry Angel she pushes her letter under his door, but in doing so inadvertently pushes it under the carpet where it remains hidden. We must accept that this could happen but we might also feel that such a stroke of bad luck at so decisive a moment in her relationship with Angel is the result of unseen forces working against her. We should note, however, that this accident is not her downfall. There was still time for her to tell Angel her past, but she chose instead to destroy the letter and acquiesce to Angel's request that she save any small talk about her 'faults and blinders' until 'some dull time' after their marriage. Ultimately, the misplaced letter had no impact on the outcome of Tess's story. Angel's excessive reaction would have been no different whether he had read her letter or listened to her oral confession. What Hardy is doing here is allowing Tess the opportunity to console herself by being fatalistic about the events in her life; he is allowing her to pity herself as a victim of fate. Many novelists, of course, are wary of coincidence in their plotting. Adam Thorpe, for instance, in *Between Each Breath* (2007), introduced a possible coincidence with a disclaimer that such could not possibly happen except in a cheap thriller or corny novel. These coincidences are frequent in Hardy's novels, but his works are neither cheap nor corny. In common with all writers, Hardy wrote for his readers and the frequent incidence of chance in his work exposed his readers to encounters with fatalistic characters from whom they could learn coping strategies. We can see that the exercise of responsibility follows enlightenment and, as Deborah Collins observed in *Thomas Hardy and His God*, readers can learn how it is possible to survive the world of random events if head and heart work together in balanced harmony.[14] In *Tess* coincidences are closely linked with characters' actions and they sometimes point to the nature of the universe. They

---

14. Deborah Collins, *Thomas Hardy and His God: A Liturgy of Unbelief* (New York, NY: St Martin's Press, 1990), p. 145.

are never the result of human wickedness; they are more often the result of what Cyril Rodd called 'the cussedness of life'.[15]

The question put in our minds by the final paragraph of *Tess* remains nonetheless: in the cussedness of life, is God toying with our emotions and lives? There is a sense in which *Hardy* toys with his readers in the framing of his novel's imagery: a series of wounded or caged birds and the dairyman's fork 'planted erect on the table like the beginning of a gallows' establish both a feeling of foreboding and an impression that we are insignificant and ineffectual when faced with the ultimate power of Hardy's President of the Immortals. Hardy's eye for misfortune and the grotesque, which led him to seek out reports of quirky accidents in local newspapers, found its way into the dark side of his novels. There is little, if any, indication of a kindly Providence in his works. Instead, Hardy builds a picture of a universe stacked against human contentment and this tragic vision, including an ambivalent deity, results in a challenge to the conventional structures of Christianity of the time. Victorian Christian morality did little to ameliorate the human lot. Indeed, it often made it worse. In *Tess*, for instance, the accusatory tone of the slogan – 'Thy damnation slumbereth not' – daubed on a board by an itinerant evangelist sank deep into Tess's heart and crushed her spirit (chapter twelve).

Hardy's campaign against Victorian churchiness lies at the heart of his vocation as a writer: he decried double standards. Angel's expectation that Tess will condone his infidelity while there is no way he will condone her less blameworthy predicament is the greatest example of this in all his novels. Angel confesses that he had 'plunged into eight-and-forty hours' dissipation with a stranger', an admission which gives Tess hope that he will now forgive her. She declares herself 'almost glad' (chapter 34). Angel is unable to respond to her confession with similar magnanimity. He cruelly says, 'Forgiveness does not apply in this case. You were one person; now you are another … how can forgiveness meet such a grotesque prestidigitation as that?' (chapter 35).

In Hardy's opinion, the Victorian Church worsened the lot of its citizens rather than improved them. As Tess's baptism of her son, Sorrow, demonstrated, it failed to face up to the realities of the modern world. Hardy was fond of the Church of England – his heart pulled

---

15. C.S. Rodd, 'God and the Novelists: 9. Thomas Hardy', *Expository Times* 110, no. 7 (1999), pp. 205-9; p. 208.

away from it only reluctantly – but he questioned the pre-eminence and power of Christianity, and he dreamed of a church stripped of its theological lumber. He longed for a church that simply reached back to the Gospel narratives, and we see this in the way that *Tess of the d'Urbervilles* rewrites a Gospel narrative. In an article in the *Times Literary Supplement*, James Mumford pointed out that the novel manipulates the biblical narrative in John chapter eight of the woman brought before her accusers. In the case of *Tess of the d'Urbervilles*, Tess's accusers arrive at intervals rather than all at once, as in John chapter eight:

> They begin to circle as early as her return from Tantridge. Her fellow parishioners are first. Angel Clare joins their ranks as soon as he discovers Tess's history. … Hardy insists on both the rank hypocrisy of the accuser … and the fact that 'Tess had *no advocate to set him right*'.[16]

Mumford points out that Hardy shows his hand only at the end of the novel when Angel is said to have thought of John's biblical narrative. Hardy 'has stretched [John chapter eight] into a story sustained over a period of time'. Overall, this provided Hardy with what Mumford called the perfect platform to explore the hypocrisy of Victorian England, in which 'Society throws its stones' and the victim is not spared.[17]

What is true of this novel is true of all novels: readers can circle up from the text into God, drill down in the text to find themselves and explore the circles around the text. Thus, novels illuminate one's understanding of the world around us. Is this how we find ourselves, our true selves? This is a question for the next chapter.

---

16. James Mumford, 'Biblical Reverses: How Thomas Hardy Plotted against God', *Times Literary Supplement*, 3 May 2019, pp. 4-5.
17. Ibid.

5

Self-Identity and Reading

Jesus, it seems, was an educated man. From the gospel of Luke's suggestion that Jesus began his ministry by reading in the Nazareth synagogue, we gather that he was literate. Since the introduction of chapter and verse to the Hebrew scriptures, the passage he read has been known to us as Isaiah 61:1-2: 'The Spirit of the Lord is upon me, because he has anointed me to bring good news to the poor. He has sent me to proclaim release to the captives and recovery of sight to the blind, to let the oppressed go free, to proclaim the year of the Lord's favour.' Having read these words, which have since been interpreted as a manifesto for his ministry, Jesus sat down and applied the passage to himself, saying, 'Today this scripture has been fulfilled in your hearing.' He became what he had read. Luke is more likely to have regarded this event as one stage in a process of self-awareness than as a sudden dawning of self-revelation. It follows several scenes in which Luke has disclosed Jesus's special identity – the boy Jesus in the temple teaching scribes, the Baptist's identification of Jesus as one who would be more powerful than he was, the voice from heaven when Jesus was baptised, and the forty days Jesus spent in the wilderness wrestling with his sense of vocation – so the words Jesus read from Isaiah serve to confirm what Luke has already shown. The scene in the synagogue and the words Jesus applied to himself prompt me to ask: when Jesus read this text, did he find himself in the reading or lose himself in it, a question that leads me to consider how modern-day readers approach their reading of a book.

Reading the scriptures of any religion in any of its sacred places is probably the most reverential form of reading there can ever be. Both the reader and hearers in a temple, mosque or church usually show utmost respect for the text, even more so than either Erasmus of Rotterdam, who reverently kissed his copy of Cicero before reading it, or Machiavelli, who dressed in his best clothes to read his favourite authors.[1] Alan Jacobs calls such submissive approaches to texts 'kenotic' reading. *Kenosis* is the theological concept of self-emptying encapsulated in Philippians 2:5-11 where St Paul expressed his understanding of the incarnation as Christ emptying himself and taking the form of a servant to be born as a man. I previously referred to Iris Murdoch's *The Unicorn*, in which Max Effingham confronts death when he slips into boggy quicksand. In immediate danger of drowning, he finds himself staring at a black globe of nothingness which is mystically filled with light. He concludes that this is 'love, to look and look until one exists no more, *this* was the love which was the same as death'.[2] As we saw in Chapter Two, Jacobs suggests that full attentiveness to a text requires prior self-annihilation of a similar order to Effingham's near-death experience. Unless as readers we empty ourselves before texts, we are not ready to become fully engaged with them.

The early nineteenth-century philosopher Schopenhauer wrote that there are two natural phases of human life, the first being to strive after existence, fighting for life and preserving oneself at all costs, and the second being to become free from the burden of existence. The first of these is, for most people, more or less accepted as a normal instinct but Schopenhauer argued that the second phase is less obvious. In this second phase, we strive to seek meaning in life rather than merely struggle for life itself.[3] Reading can be part of this search for meaning and full self-immersion in what we read demonstrates a desire to break free from the burden of living a meaningless existence. In his 'Reading for Life' project, Philip Davis discovered that realist novels, in particular, can immerse readers in the mundane secular lives they portray so effectively that questions assisting their actual living in the real world are brought to the surface. Troubles experienced by fictional characters in realist novels can help readers facing

---

1. Fischer, *A History of Reading*, p. 218.
2. Murdoch, *The Unicorn*, p. 198.
3. Davis, *Reading for Life*, p. 15.

comparable troubles to make sense of their actual experiences. Thus, reading such novels can become a form of 'implicit psychotherapy'.[4] This therapy is the potential reward for perfect attentiveness to, and perfect love for, whatever one reads selflessly.

I suggest that this attentiveness to the text and love for it begins with a form of lostness. During the coronavirus pandemic of the early 2020s I found myself watching more television dramas than usual and I was less selective in advance about my television viewing than previously. I realised, however, that, unless I lost myself in either the characters or the situation early in the programme, I soon gave up watching: the plot had not hooked me in and I did not empathise with the characters. So it is with novels. To enter a novel's world, I must first dislocate myself from my world, lose where I am and find my way into the time and place where the novel is located. I must leave behind current cares and concerns, empty my mind and open myself to the new world the novel offers. Reverence for the text may be too strong a word, but I must certainly have sufficient respect or regard for a book to submit myself to it. Opening a book requires an open mind.

Mark Edmundson's argument for high-quality literary teaching reminds us that, according to both Plato and Aristotle, philosophy begins with a sense of wonder and, according to Wittgenstein, it begins with confusion.[5] In other words, marvelling at the world we live in can cause us to think more deeply about it and serious thinking can result from a sense of being lost. We read best when we become ignorant again, lost, for example, with Dickens's Pip in the overgrown churchyard where he meets the fearful Magwitch and where his expectations and adventures begin. We read *Great Expectations* best when, having made ourselves ignorant again at the first page, we open minds and hearts to discover Pip's world and explore it with him. In such ignorance there lies the beginning of potential change as we become more knowing. We first lose ourselves so that we may find ourselves.

We begin reading by emptying ourselves but we soon rediscover ourselves.

* * *

---

4. Ibid., p. 16.
5. Edmundson, *Why Read?*, p. 33.

The experience of lostness on entering a novel's world could be compared to walking into a hall of mirrors, not like a hall of mirrors as at Versailles but a hall of amusement arcade mirrors of manifold distorting shapes and sizes. In each mirror the onlooker is reflected differently: in one a distended body, in another a shrunken body, in one a swollen head, in another, a pin head and so on. Here, the hall represents the book in its entirety, and the range of mirrors the range of pluriform insights a single book can offer. According to Jacobs, this can be thought of as quixotic, after Cervantes's Don Quixote who was capable of interpreting every experience within the context of his own imagined chivalric world.[6] A reader's comparable ability to interpret what he or she sees in fictional characters' experiences, in such a way that they give insights into the reader's actual lived experiences, is informative and life enhancing. Jacobs writes of books becoming mirrors where readers see reflections of their own imperfections and struggles, as well as their potentialities. Some of the mirrors are dangerous because they can deceive readers and feed arrogant behaviour. Others generously reflect kinder images that encourage both a better understanding of oneself and a better disposition towards other people. Jacobs warns, therefore, that quixotic reading must always be highly attentive, so that readers carefully avoid misleading delusion and open up the possibility of improved self-awareness.

You might find that another image that helps you understand this process of self-discovery in a novel is the one I described in the previous chapter, that of Teresa of Avila's interior journey through seven stages. Here the soul is seen as a complex dwelling, a castle of transparent crystal in which one room after another leads towards the centre where the king lives. We need a map of ourselves to make this journey and, when we complete the journey, we have found our true self. We find the king (of the castle!). Our journey through stages of interiority brings us to the place where we find both God and ourselves. Perhaps, like Christian in Bunyan's *The Pilgrim's Progress*, the journey is full of distractions, including a vanity fair of mirrored halls, but diversions like these make interesting reading, to say the least. Having successfully navigated all distractions, we then reach the place of knowing ourselves. Perhaps for the first time.

---

6. Jacobs, *A Theology of Reading*, p. 91.

Josie Billington observes that what is going on when we come to know ourselves in what we read is 'two-way' reading. I am outside the book reading it from my external location, while the book simultaneously reads me from within.[7] Perhaps this is what a somewhat puzzling verse in the book of Psalms is alluding to in saying: 'Once God has spoken, twice have I heard this' (Psalm 62:11). Reading texts is two-directional in that, when we examine words, we examine ourselves and we examine ourselves using words. Billington illustrates this with an account of a participant in a read-aloud group who found that engaging with Ebeneezer Scrooge's encounter with Christmas Past in Dickens's *A Christmas Carol* returned him to his childhood school. In the story Scrooge reverted to his former self as a lonely boy reading by a feeble fire and wept at his memory of the experience. The reading group participant comments that Scrooge, who when he was a boy was incapable of feeling lonely, only now weeps for his loneliness. As the boy was forgotten by others, so the man has forgotten himself. Billington observes that, in this scene, Scrooge, as a hardened adult, sees himself as an innocent child in a way that reanimates the older man. Billington calls this the story's 'second voice' and its 'deep structure'. On this point, she is aligned with the novelist Marilynne Robinson whom she cites as having spoken of texts having 'inner voices'.[8] This inner thinking is unlimited and the inner voice is uninhibited.

Readers are simultaneously outside and inside the text. Billington says, 'The reader is still ... audience and witness to the text, which exists *outside*; but at the same time, the mind is the realizer of its own sudden inner message'.[9] The hall of mirrors we enter when we open the pages of a novel triggers echoes that we recognise within ourselves. We see, hear and feel ourselves afresh in our reading to such an extent that fiction helps us navigate our actual social world by offering simulated opportunities for us to discover new knowledge and fresh understanding of self and others, thus sharpening our social awareness and ethical behaviour. I stress the word 'offering' in the previous statement, because I do not want it to be thought that I assume that readers are necessarily better people than non-readers.

---

7. Josie Billington, *Is Literature Healthy?* (Oxford: Oxford University Press, 2016), p. 125.
8. Ibid., p.126.
9. Ibid. (Billington's italics).

This is clearly not so. Reading does *not* necessarily make us better people. It has the *potential* to do so but not all readers accept what reading offers. Some people responsible for evil acts have been avid readers and keen appreciators of the other arts! If reading is to be self-improving, we must be open to triggers in the text that teach us more of ourselves.

Do we need, though, to learn different lessons about ourselves at different stages of life? Helen Taylor launched into writing a book about why women read novels to find out how important fiction was to her and to what extent it had become incorporated into her own life story and journey. The research she conducted amongst women readers shows that many had reading lives that were divided into several chapters. One, for instance, read Émile Zola as a self-confessed morose teenager, Isabelle Allende and Angela Carter as a young adult, trapped in a job she did not enjoy, and crime fiction in later life at the point when she had come to realise how finite life is.[10] Many of her respondents described variations on this theme. Taylor compares this with what she calls the cliché that people have a soundtrack to their lives made up of their significant musical choices. This, indeed, is the basis for one of the longest running programmes on British radio, *Desert Island Discs*, introduced on the BBC Forces Programme (part of BBC Home Service) in 1942 by Roy Plumley and still going today on BBC Radio 4. Guests are invited to imagine that they have been cast away on an uninhabited island and to select eight pieces of music they would want to take with them. Almost always the guests choose music associated with their past lives or with a person with whom they have shared some part of their lives. I guess I am not the only listener who wonders how I would make my choices if I ever needed to.

There is a similar section in *Saturday Live* on BBC Radio 4. It is entitled 'Inheritance Tracks'. Here a guest talks first about a cherished piece of 'inherited' music. It might be a tune learnt from a parent, sung in the childhood home or taught by a teacher. Then the guest turns attention to the track he or she wants to bequeath to others. Again, almost always, both the inherited music and the music to be bequeathed have strong links with the guest's lived experiences – and, again, I wonder what I would choose for my inheritance track. There

---

10. Helen Taylor, *Why Women Read Fiction: The Stories of Our Lives* (Oxford: Oxford University Press, 2019), pp. 227-28.

is too much music in my life to reduce to eight desert island discs or one inheritance track.

In actual fact, I am currently facing a similar exercise in the case of books. Sometime, quite soon, I am expecting to move out of a manse with yards of bookshelves after many decades of accumulating books. I shall need to reduce my collection to fit into a more affordable retirement home while leaving room there for us and life's other requisites. How do I choose what to take from the collection that represents a lifetime of reading theology, novels and poetry? What will go into the boxes for the charity shops? Many difficult decisions lie ahead because, without doubt, each book could make a case for going with me because, if I accept the opinions of most of Taylor's respondents, each book could be regarded as a chapter in my life's journey. They map my life.

On the other hand, some of the women who completed Taylor's questionnaire thought that the idea of lives divided into chapters was too neat. Our lives are not linear in that fashion. Several years ago, I decided one summer to reread many of the books I had read during my schooldays. The experiment was revelatory in several ways: some books I remembered fondly had become a chore to read, whilst others about which I had happy memories were rich enough to yield fresh, life-enriching insights. What matters for the fulfilled human being is that we can write the stories of our multi-faceted and multi-layered lives over, across and within our reading-lives whereby what we read illuminates what we experience.

John Cottingham said that 'there is always a story to be told about how I became what I now am, how I learn from my past mistakes, and the destination at which I am now aiming' but this is only possible if we are able to see life as a 'morally integrated whole'.[11] This is a much more robust understanding of the nature of human existence than life as a series of episodic chapters. Cottingham's contention is that integrity of life is essential to secure the health of the soul, the wellbeing of our very selves, making the prayer of Psalm 86:11 – 'Give me, O Lord, an undivided heart' – a prayer that lies at the centre of well-lived and fulfilled spirituality. It is a prayer for psychological and moral unity. The struggle for wholeness, or unity of selfhood, is the goal of spiritual practice. Cottingham notes that this quest for wholeness of being is central to the biblical narrative and to Christian teaching. He reminds us that the Gospels speak of the importance

---

11. Cottingham, *In Search of the Soul*, p. 20.

of 'securing the health of the precious *soul* or *self*'[12] or 'finding one's *true* self'[13] and that nothing, not even gaining the whole world, is sufficient to compensate for the loss of self. To illustrate his point, he refers to Jesus's parable of the prodigal son who 'comes to himself' in a moment of reawakening after having left home for a distant land and squandering his inheritance. Cottingham comments that the Dominican writer, Timothy Radcliffe, regarded the prodigal's decision to return home as being the same as rediscovering his true self, inasmuch as his exile in a distant land was as much an exile from his true identity as a son and a brother as it was exile from his family. Radcliffe had said that the prodigal could only find himself again when he was with family. This loss of self, said Cottingham, is what Kierkegaard called 'sickness unto death', the loss of one's soul.[14]

Now, in writing this spirituality for booklovers, I am suggesting that we might consider how the books we read map our lifetime quest for wholeness and integrity of being, and our search for fullness of life. We might, therefore, pause and ask: what eight books would I take to a desert island? What novels have been the most-valued and trusted companions on my walk through this life? Which shall I take with me when my home cannot accommodate a large library? I, for instance, have discovered while writing this book that one story I could not live without is the parable of the prodigal son. I have not been able to resist referring to it three or four times in this book and this has made me realise how central Luke's brilliant storytelling is to my understanding of the Christian faith and Christian spirituality. It is perhaps the last story I would want to hear. I might even want to carry a copy of it with me as I approach the pearly gates!

Following the example of John Wesley, whose journals reveal that his claim to be a man of one book (by which he meant the Bible, of course) was far from the truth because they reveal him to be well-read and widely read, I have kept a reading journal since 1988, this being what Methodist ministers call 'my year of travel', the year I began itinerant circuit ministry. Some would think this is a nerdy thing to do. I honestly cannot remember why I began to record the titles and the authors of the books I read, but, whatever the original reason, the benefit of it now is that I have a record of what one of Helen

---

12. Ibid., pp. 20-21 (Cottingham's italics).
13. Ibid., p.109 (Cottingham's italics).
14. Ibid., p.109.

Self-Identity and Reading 69

Taylor's respondents called a 'reading life'. I can examine this record and trace there my development of thought as I have travelled. I can see more clearly than I would otherwise have been able to do which thinkers and writers have exercised the greater influence on me. My reading journal shows me how I have changed. It traces my quest for wholeness and integrity which is the lifetime quest of every person aware of being in any sense spiritual. This record of my reading life helps me to understand why I am who I am.

In about 1566, Giuseppe Arcimboldo, an artist employed in the Habsburg court of Maximilian II in Prague, painted a picture of a man made of books. Arcimboldo's main employment was the design of stained-glass windows, tapestries and costumes, but he amused himself making surreal portraits comprised of fruit, flowers and other natural objects. The portrait comprised of books is appropriately titled 'The Librarian'. Whether or not it portrays an actual person is, to me, a matter of unnecessary scholarly speculation. The painting becomes more interesting if we think of it as representing everyone.

In *Portable Magic*, Emma Smith neatly describes the painting:

> A man constructed from books. His shock of white hair is actually a concertina of open pages, the straight line of his right arm is formed of a large orange volume. His ribs, or the folds of his doublet, are suggested by a horizontal stack of end-on similar, pale vellum-bound books; a flutter of protruding paper bookmarks indicates his delicate fingers; and a floating ribbon bookmark traces the outline of his left ear. His soft, tufted beard is a book duster formed of marten tails; his spectacles are made of the keys to the chests in which books were stored before the widespread adoption of open book-shelves in the eighteenth century.[15]

This is a visual depiction of how we are all made up of the books we have studied, read and loved – or, indeed, disagreed with, disliked or rejected. Even books we have not read can be part of who we are. Some who visit my study ask whether I have read all the books on the shelves. The truth is that more time has been spent dusting some of them than has been spent reading them, and yet they are still

---

15. Emma Smith, *Portable Magic: A History of Books and Their Readers* (London: Allen Lane, 2022), p. 224.

part of who I am in that, for since-forgotten reasons, I once bought those books because they had some significance or interest for me. Moreover, some of those lingering on the shelves still unread were gifts, from people for whom I have much greater fondness than I have for their choice of books. The unread gift remains on the shelf as a memory of a friendship. In all these ways and more, the books on my shelves, the books I no longer have any room for and the books recorded in my reading journal have made me what I am.

In conclusion, I offer you a spiritual exercise you might want to do before you close this chapter. Think back over your reading history and identify a book, a genre of literature or a shortlist of books that belong to a particular part of your life, for example, childhood, adolescence, college days, early adulthood, parenthood, middle age, perhaps a breakdown of relationships, later years and so on. Why these books at these times? What did they teach you about yourself? How did they help you find your true self? What did you learn about God through this literature? Were these lessons fleeting or long-lasting? Would you go back to these books now?

Having explored these questions you might then want to consider whether this exercise helps you identify distinct chapters in your life; or do the chapters, instead, overlap so that lessons learnt in one stage are not lost in others, meaning that life's chapters are more of an accumulating continuum than a linear series? In the end, what does this show you about who and what you are?

6

Silent Conversation with the Absent Other

On a visit to London's Victoria and Albert Museum I came across a collection of medieval English alabaster carvings, among which the Holy Trinity is one of the most popular subjects. One of the finest is a late fifteenth-century example in which God the Father, with hands raised in blessing, looks down on God the Son. Angels collect redeeming blood in a chalice as it flows from Christ's hands and feet. Even at first sight one notices an obvious absence: where in the carving is the Holy Spirit represented? Closer inspection revealed that the Holy Spirit is represented by a hole. This, however, was not the original intention. Originally the Spirit was carved separately and secured by a dowel from the main panel so that it protruded from the panel. Over time the carving and the dowel have been lost and all that can be seen is a hole. I am stimulated by the thought that the Holy Spirit is represented by a hole. After all, in the Judaeo-Christian tradition, the Holy of Holies where God dwelt was an empty space and the risen Christ is represented by an empty tomb. Nothingness represents the ultimate Something.

Since the middle years of the twentieth century, when Karl Barth contended that we can only know of God what God chooses to reveal, one of the key theological questions has been: what can we know about God? Closely related to this question are others: what can we say about God? What can we use to represent God? For some, the answer to these questions is 'Very little'. The late twentieth-century hymn writer, Elizabeth Cosnett, posed similar questions in the first verse of one of her hymns:

> Can we by searching find out God
> or formulate his ways?
> Can numbers measure what he is
> or words contain his praise?

She implied negative answers to these questions until, in the last verse of the hymn, she switched and concluded that the answer would have been 'No' if God had not 'broken in upon our search' in the birth, life and death of Christ. Here she concurs with Barth: we would not know God if God did not reveal Godself to us.

This sense of dependence on revelation for knowing God highlights the existence of two opposing, but complimentary, approaches to theology and spirituality. Using terms derived from Greek, these are the apophatic and cataphatic ways, otherwise known by Latin terms: the *via negativa* and the *via affirmativa*. This chapter discussing absence and otherness in literature and spirituality, and exploring the concept of reading as a silent conversation with the absent, focusses on the first of these ways of talking about and relating to God, the apophatic way or *via negativa*.

The cataphatic approach to theology and spirituality uses images, names and language to help us conceptualise God: for instance, the Lord is my shepherd, our Father who is in heaven, the Lord is our refuge, our comforter and our strength, and so on. All these are positive statements which use unambivalent images to state who God is for us. These can be biblical images – indeed, they often are – but they can also derive from more recent insights using contemporary images.

The suggestion made by the apophatic approach that we cannot make positive statements about God appears to contradict and oppose the cataphatic way, but the truth of the matter is that the apophatic way is not an alternative approach but a related and complementary way. In short, it avoids conceptualising God and seeks to encounter and experience the unknowable, ineffable God. To understand this approach we need to look back to one of the Cappadocian Fathers of the fourth century, Gregory, who was bishop of Nyssa until his death in 395. Central to his theology was the notion that the Christian life is a progression through stages of purification by which passions are defeated and the image of God restored in us. This progression involves illumination in which we eventually see God in the purified mirror of our souls. To reach the highest state of purity, the soul longs more and more for God until it learns that God is totally and unutterably different from (or Other than) all created things. God transcends all creation. Gregory recalled that Moses entered a dark cloud when he met God on Sinai and picked up on this image of divine darkness to describe the pilgrim's progress: we must enter this divine darkness, having stripped away all intellectual obstacles and sensual impressions, before we can draw close to God. This close proximity to God is achieved when prayer is pure and communion with God is fulfilled without recourse to words or images of any kind. For Gregory, this state of bliss was when a Christian knew nothing but the God who lies beyond all that is created. Thus, apophatic theology and spirituality move towards God by asserting that God is not any of the things we call God. We begin with the physical creation we are part of, where we find what is intelligible to us, but we move from this limited and compromised understanding to the deeper knowledge of God and union with God that are found in the divine darkness that lies beyond human conceptualisation.

A Buddhist story of the fish and the turtle tells of a fish that knew nothing but water. One day it met a turtle shortly after returning from a visit to dry land. The fish refused to believe where the turtle had been because it knew nothing about land. 'Is it wet', it asked. 'No', the turtle replied. 'Is it soft, fresh and cool?' 'No.' 'Is it clear so that light can come through it? Is it yielding and does it flow in streams? Does it rise in waves and foam?' To each question, the turtle replied in the negative. Despairing, the fish pooh-poohed the turtle's experience and declared that if dry land was none of these things, then it is nothing. The turtle dismissed the fish as silly for concluding that something it has never known must be nothing simply because it has never known it. This tale has been used in several ways. We can use it here as a memorable illustration of the inability of theology to define God. The turtle was unable to say anything about dry land beyond saying what it is not, because of the fish's limited experience. Similarly, often the most we can say about God is what God is not.

Apophatic spirituality emphasises silence, darkness, passivity and absence of images. It takes us beyond what we can grasp through the cataphatic way because any human expression of God is unavoidably and radically inadequate, like the fish's understanding of dry land.

God is 'neither this nor that' and is best known in obscurity. Gregory of Nyssa is not the only classical theologian holding such views. We can also turn to the Syrian monk known only by his pseudonym, Pseudo-Dionysius the Areopagite, who flourished around 500 CE and who wrote of the divine names by which we can know God. Because nothing truly expresses God because God is beyond all being, Pseudo-Dionysius moved on from this affirmation of names for God to promote the need for us to abandon our senses and intellect in an intentional and disciplined manner so that we can lose ourselves in the divine darkness. Paradoxically, we are able to find enlightenment in this divine darkness. In the thirteenth century, the German mystic, Meister Eckhart, took a similar apophatic route, and he is a useful and more accessible source for modern readers than Gregory or Pseudo-Dionysius because of the work of the American priest and theologian, Matthew Fox.

Among more radical thinkers of the late twentieth and early twenty-first centuries, the apophatic approach has been on trend. Michael Sells studied the writings and lives of several mystics and argued that they employed a 'language of unsaying' in which all propositions cancel each other out to create what he called 'anarchic moments'. The examples he gives are those of John Scotus Eriugena speaking in the ninth century of the nothingness of God, the French mystic Marguerite Porete's annihilation of self, and Eckhart's letting go of God to find God.[1] These anarchic moments are creative, revelatory and sanctifying, and draw the individual deeper into the dark holiness of God. Such mysticism deconstructs divine power. It takes little imagination to relate these notions with sayings of Christ in the Gospels about denying self to follow him and with Paul's notion of dying in order to live.

Better known to British Christians is Don Cupitt, who argued for a surrender to mysticism on the premise that mystical Christianity breaks down the dominant strain of institutional, patriarchal and hierarchical emphasis on power. In the rapture of mystical religious experience, he wrote, 'the soul is dissolved [and] drowned. ... God pours out his spirit. Grace erupts into the soul like a jet of warm

---

1. Michael Sells, *Mystical Languages of Unsaying* (Chicago: University of Chicago Press, 1994), p. 209.

liquid. It tastes sweet.'² Again, surrender of self leads to absorption into God where the individual is lost and found in wonder and love.

What I hope to have shown in these brief comments is that the apophatic approach to spirituality is naturally drawn to the mystery, inaccessibility and transcendence of God. It accentuates the holy (and wholly) Otherness of God who is always beyond and above us. It emphasises the mystical approach to prayer which calls for the suspension of senses, concepts and self-image through techniques such as meditation. It affirms 'clouds of unknowing' (to employ a familiar term coined by an anonymous fourteenth-century English spiritual writer). Both Eastern Orthodox and Quaker Christians are familiar with these ideas, although a Christian from either of these traditions would find the ideas expressed and practised quite differently in the other tradition. In short, apophatic spirituality takes us beyond and outside ourselves into the Otherness of God, via self-emptying into nothingness.

The argument of this chapter is that we can use fiction to explore this self-emptying into the Otherness of God. This is because fiction has the knack of putting on the page what exists exclusively in the mind of its author and its readers. It deals with the 'great absence that is like a presence' as R.S. Thomas described God, awareness of whom compelled him to pray without any hope of a reply (as he put it in his poem, 'The Absence', published in 1978).

Forty years ago, the autobiographical account of a young woman who entered a convent at the age of seventeen to take vows of poverty, chastity and obedience three years later, who was sent to Oxford University after five years to prepare to teach in one of the order's schools, but who left the order two years later before completing her degree, became a publishing sensation in Britain. The book was *Through the Narrow Gate: A Nun's Story* (1997); the author was Karen Armstrong. Armstrong's experience had exploded her capacity to believe in God. Yet, ironically, she has since achieved fame as a writer on religious themes and a biographer of religious figures. Her experience in the convent was alienating; it alienated her from others, from herself and from whoever God might be. Despite expecting to enter into deep intimacy with God in the convent, she experienced nothing but the absence of God. It might be thought ironic that,

---

2. Don Cupitt, *Mysticism after Modernity* (Oxford: Blackwell, 1998), pp. 43-44.

despite experiencing only God's absence, almost all of Armstrong's later books trace other people's experiences of the presence of God in their lives. I think the paradox of Armstrong's career is because when we talk about God (that is, when we do theology or practise spirituality) we are dealing with absent presence, or present absence. We should remember that there are two types of absence. One is where someone or something might be present but is not, and the other is when someone never has been, never will be and never could be present. When we speak of the absence of God, we are not speaking of this second type of absence. God could be present but is not. This is the paradox fiction explores.

Of course, there is another paradox (or irony, depending on how you see it) associated with reading. Readers withdraw from others to a quiet place, avoiding distraction, not to be shut up in their own minds (as we would if we stepped aside to think for a while), but to search the book they read for the company of others and to connect with them in an intimate way. Through reading we connect with other people including the author, fictional characters and any real people the characters might remind us of; we connect with the larger world in that the book takes us from our own time and place to other times and places; and we potentially connect with God. All this is possible whether the reader is a child who hides under the bedsheets to read or an adult who buries his or her head in a book (as the common expression has it). When we read, we *want* to meet someone other than ourselves. Nevertheless, for the sake of this chapter, I ask you to notice that whoever we meet in a book is *absent*. Reading is an act of withdrawal from the present world to engage with absence.

Augustine was one of the first to notice this. In *De Trinitate*, Augustine recognised that words are not identical to the things to which they refer; rather, they are signs that we use to refer to things in their absence. The signs point to something else; the marks on the page stand in for absence. For Augustine, the letters of the alphabet were invented to be 'signs of sounds' that were also signs of the things we think; they had been devised so that we could converse even with the absent. Whatever the words refer to is not there. The words are substitutes for an absent reality. This distinction between the sign and its referent is, of course, unavoidable, and Augustine argued that this distancing between sign and referent is also a characteristic of the relationship between humanity and the divine since the Fall. According to Augustine, since Adam and Eve were evicted from Eden in the creation myth, the best communication with the divine we can hope for is indirect. We no longer see God face to face, and there is no direct language available for successful communication between God and fallen humanity. Even our talk about God is compromised by this distancing.

Daniel Coleman proposed that this presence-in-absence which is fundamental to reading is precisely parallel to the experience of prayer. In both reading and praying we reach out to an Other who is beyond both our grasp and comprehension.[3] We pray to One who is there and not there, in much the same way as we meet fictional characters in novels who are also simultaneously there and not there. When we read *Middlemarch*, for instance, we bump along with made-up characters who become real for us, and we meet in them (and in their creator) people who differ from us. As Jeanette Winterson once explained her love of literature, reading is 'a life-long collision with minds not like your own'.[4] So, reading feels less like an escape under metaphorical bedsheets from life's trials and tribulations and more like a pressing and crucial dimension of living in the moment, by which we encounter life's realities.

Time now to demonstrate the spirituality of absence and apophasis in literature with an extended example; and I think the best way to do this is to spend some time with a book at whose centre there is a foreboding, almost silent, emptiness which I can never avoid associating with the 'sound of sheer silence' which formed Elijah's encounter with God in first Kings chapter nineteen. The example I turn to is the novel of 1924 I have lived with since undergraduate days when it served as a core text in my literature studies: E.M. Forster's *A Passage to India*, familiar to many through David Lean's faithful interpretation on film in 1984.

A Passage to India is a novel with a gap in the middle. The gap is a cave in the Marabar Hills where an ill-defined calamity occurs. At the outset of the novel, a young English woman, Adela Quested, goes to India, during the time of the Raj, to meet up with the man she intends to marry, accompanied by an elderly friend, Mrs Moore. The marriage never happens. Aziz, a local Muslim doctor who has befriended Mrs Moore, organises a charabanc trip to have a picnic at the Marabar Caves. These ancient caves, of some significance to

---

3. Coleman, *In Bed with the Word*, p. 72.
4. Quoted in Taylor, *Why Women Read Fiction*, p. 9.

the Jain religion, are utterly empty. Each cave is a black hole with an unearthly echo reducing all sounds to a monotonous 'boum'. Both the loftiest poetry and vile cursing are reduced to this nothingness of an echo. Inside the caves, both Adela and Mrs Moore undergo a crisis, the precise nature of which is never fully revealed. Adela breaks down in terror and accuses Aziz of attempted rape, whilst Mrs Moore finds that the echo in some way unsettles her and she soon leaves India to go back to England. She dies on the return voyage. Aziz is brought to court but the trial is chaotic and collapses at the last minutes when Adela realises that she was mistaken to accuse him. Thus, the puzzle at the heart of the novel – what actually happened in the caves – is never solved.

In recent years literary critics have tended to approach *A Passage to India* either as a post-colonialist text concerned with problems of race and colonialism or as a queer text exploring homoerotic male friendships. In his introduction to the life and work of Forster, Nicholas Royle sees value in both these approaches, first, because they alert readers to the intricacies and complexities of Forster's writing and, second, because they make us aware that we cannot read this novel without finding ourselves bound up in its imperialist, racial and sexual politics.[5] In an interesting, if brief, analysis of the vocabulary Forster employs, Royle shows that Forster often plays with the word 'queer'. To give only a few examples: Adela is introduced as a queer girl; Aziz regards the British headmaster of a local Indian college, Fielding, as a queer chap; Godbole sings queer songs; what happens at the caves is queer; Mrs Moore becomes disagreeable and queer after visiting the caves; and India is called the queer nation. The resulting effect is that, in addition to the humour in the novel when we laugh at the characters' often peculiar behaviour, we also detect that the entire text is strangely mysterious. Indeed, at its heart there is an unexplained mystery.

I do not question the validity of these dominant critical approaches but I find that the strangeness of *A Passage to India* means that I find I must take a different approach. For me, it is primarily a spiritual and theological text. For me, it is a novel set in a deeply religious environment exploring the mystery of people as spiritual beings. Forster presents India as a confluence of religions: Aziz is Muslim, Godbole is Hindu, the caves are Jain and the English characters in

---

5. Nicholas Royle, *E.M. Forster* (Plymouth: Northcote House, 1999), p. 73.

their various ways represent 'poor talkative little Christianity' (as Mrs Moore puts it). The mysterious, unexplained events of the novel are a crucible in which these faiths are put to the test. The interplay of these faiths forms an integral part of the relationships between the characters while friendships are forged; and this interplay continues to be important when the relationships, in time, fall apart.

With regard to the novel as a spiritual and religious text, there is another significant recurring word in Forster's vocabulary range. It is the word 'extraordinary'. Royle notes that it is present in the novel's opening sentence: 'Except for the Marabar Caves – and they are twenty miles off – the city of Chandrapore presents nothing extraordinary.' He also suggests that this sentence carries the novel's entire weight:

> This sentence has a cavernous quality: it implies knowledge of something 'extraordinary', but in an ironic, negative mode; it implies a clear sense of place (the phrase 'twenty miles off' establishes the location of the narrative voice), but also a peculiar collapsing of space (although 'twenty miles off', the Caves are nevertheless somehow part of the city, part of what it may have to 'present').[6]

The word 'extraordinary' hints at something remarkable or wonderful, something special and unusual, something beyond or outside order. Whatever is extraordinary about the caves unsettles both interior minds and external lives.

Royle demonstrates how the word 'extraordinary' echoes throughout the entire length of the novel. After its first appearance in the opening sentence, it is repeated in the closing sentence of the first chapter. It recurs just after Aziz has invited Mrs Moore to accompany him on a visit to the caves when it transpires that he has never visited them and that he does not know what to say about them. Not knowing what to say, Aziz asks Professor Godbole to say what is special about the caves but Godbole's unfocussed chatter in reply leads the narrator to observe that Godbole failed to reveal anything that was extraordinary about them.[7] The word 'extraordinary' returns at the moment of revelation when Adela realises that she had made a terrible mistake in making allegations against Aziz: 'An

---

6. Ibid., p. 78.
7. Ibid., p. 75.

extraordinary expression was on her face, half relief, half horror.'⁸ Later she describes her own conduct as extraordinary. Royle contends that extraordinary as a word 'encapsulates ... both the strangeness of the Marabar Caves and of the text in which they are to be found' and that it is somehow 'outside the order of "human speech"'.⁹

Forster always refused to explain the extraordinary events in the Marabar Caves. When asked what happened in the caves, Forster wrote to his friend Goldsworthy Lowes Dickinson in June 1924 that it was '*either* a man, *or* the supernatural, *or* an illusion' (with the conjunctions italicised in the original to emphasise the range of possible explanations). The uncertainty of what happened there is, he said, a trick.¹⁰ Forster chose not to reveal what had happened in order to maintain the mystery; he certainly did not want to end it. It remains extraordinary.

Because *A Passage to India* was Forster's final foray into long fiction, the last novel he wrote despite living and working in the literary world for a further 35 years and more, Royle describes it as his last exploration of 'deferral as the condition of reading and meaning'.¹¹ The novel is Forster's final exposition of indirectness and ambivalence as the essential condition of our spiritual lives in relation to God who, I suggest, is no less than *the* Extraordinary, the strange absent who is always present. As Royle puts it, 'the significance of what happens in the Marabar Caves continues to echo, inscribing itself in the "not-yet" with which the novel closes'.¹² This not-yet expresses the deferral and contingency of apophatic spirituality, in which we must wait for revelation and understanding.

I think that this, rather than the politics of race and sex, was Forster's intended field of exploration in the novel, and I am encouraged in this view by Peter Burra's introduction to the 1942 Everyman edition. Here Burra said that Forster had set out to define the difference between real life and the life presented to us by the arts. The work of fiction is to tidy up life's experiences and put them in some sort of order that makes sense. It takes the bits and pieces of our stories and brings

---

8. Ibid., p. 207.
9. Ibid., pp. 80-81.
10. The letter is discussed at greater length in P.N. Furbank, *E.M. Forster: A Life*, 2 vols (London: Secker & Warburg, 1977-78), Vol. 2, p. 124.
11. Royle, *Forster*, p. 83.
12. Ibid., p. 84.

them into coherent narratives. Real life is much messier and more disjointed. In real life, the human predicament can be difficult to understand and meaning can be hard to find. In *Aspects of the Novel* in which Forster discussed aspects of his art, he addressed the matter of real life's messiness and said that novelists introduce patterns and rhythm to their narratives to suggest there is meaning to human life. These linking motifs provide meaningful shape and content to life which, in reality, we can receive as little more than 'one damned thing after another'. Forster's *A Passage to India* presents life's messiness in several ways, but especially in the unexplained events at the caves, the chaos of the trial, the inadequacy of both western and eastern religions to account for life's mysteries, and the unachieved aims of so many of the characters. Adela's quest for a husband is unfulfilled, Mrs Moore dies on her way back to England and the desired friendship between Fielding and Aziz is prevented by horses that swerve apart in the final scene. Yet the novel's treatment of its central mystery and its overarching spirituality suggest that mess and chaos do not have the last word.

Forster uses apophasis – silence and the absence of imagery – to achieve the sense that there is always more to say. In Elizabeth Lowry's rereading of *A Passage to India* for an article in the *Times Literary Supplement*, she wrote:

> silence is what *A Passage to India* gives us. All its clues and links are a diversion in the quest for meaning, a detour, that lead us to the central revelation of the book: that there is none. At the heart of *A Passage to India* there is a hole. Various philosophic statements have been attributed to its central mystery, the mystery of what happens in the Marabar, variously framed in Hindu, Jain or Jungian terms. Its final message is one of hope; its final message is one of despair. But its final message is no such thing. It is, quite literally, nothing.[13]

This is similar to an observation the novelist Sebastian Faulks made that the most critical points in Hardy's *Tess of the d'Urbervilles*, in other words when the action moves on, come in moments of silence:

---

13. Elizabeth Lowry, 'Listening for the Echo: Re-reading A Passage to India', *Times Literary Supplement*, 5 June 2020, p. 9.

> The three key moments in this novel all occur when nothing happens: the first when Angel does not ask Tess to dance; the second when she has told him her secret and asks if he can love her and he makes no reply; and the third when once again he shows what he believes by remaining silent [when she asks whether they will meet again after they are dead].[14]

Perhaps the most creative and revelatory moments of our lives are when all is silent, when God seems absent, and when spirituality is arid, for then we are forced to our knees by circumstances and must dig deep.

Nothingness is not only what we encounter in *A Passage to India*'s Marabar caves but also the key to the text. Nothingness characterises the caves: 'Nothing is inside them, they were sealed up before the creation of pestilence or treasure; if mankind grew curious and excavated, nothing, nothing would be added to the sum of good or evil.'[15] Forster carefully distinguishes nothingness from absence. As we saw above, absence implies presence: the absent schoolchild when the roll is being called is not there, but *is* somewhere else. Moreover, absence implies that the gap can be filled: the school desk is not taken away because the child is absent because the teacher hopes it will be needed the next day. Absence holds the promise of possible fulfilment and possible presence. Forster flags this up in a strange scene early in the novel which comes to serve as an image for the perpetual spiritual quest. Adela and Mrs Moore are bewildered when, unprompted, Professor Godbole sings a Hindu raga. The song, like real life in the raw, has no rhythm or pattern. Their ears, more accustomed to European music, 'soon lost any clue, and wandered in a maze of noises, none harsh or unpleasant, none intelligible'.[16] Godbole explains his song: 'It was a religious song. I placed myself in the position of a milkmaiden. I say to Shri Krishna, "Come! Come to me only." The God refuses to come.' Mrs Moore asks whether the God comes in response to some other song, but Godbole's reply is in

---

14. Sebastian Faulks, *Faulks on Fiction: The Secret Life of the Novel* (London: BBC Books, 2011), p. 155.
15. E.M. Forster, *A Passage to India*, (Harmondsworth: Penguin Modern Classics, 1961), p. 125.
16. Ibid., p. 77.

the negative: 'He refuses to come. I say to Him, Come, come, come, come, originate, come. He neglects to come (78).'[17] This episode comes before the visit to the caves and Godbole's unintelligible song, issuing an invitation which is never answered, serves to prepare readers to discover the effect the caves have on any noise, whether it be beautiful music or a throat-clearing grunt: whatever is said in the caves is reduced to 'the same monotonous noise … utterly dull'.[18] The episode also describes the futility of divine invocation: God will not be found by searching. Our repeated failure to complete the quest means that we are on a perpetual pilgrimage. As J.P. Williams would have it: 'Even if it appears that we have reached the destination of our earthly pilgrimage, we never completely and finally *arrive*.'[19] In this sense, each of us, like Godbole, is like the Celtic saint, Columba, who clambered into a coracle and let the wind, the waves and the Spirit take him to wherever he landed until it felt time to move on again. We do not find our rest until we rest at the end – in God.

There is much more to *A Passage to India* than the scene in the caves. Even so, the entire novel has a similar effect on the reader as the caves had on their visitors. As Lowry said, 'You go into a sacred cave, expecting a revelation, and the answer is "boum". You go to the novel, expecting an interpretation of reality, and the answer is "boum".'[20] The assertions of literature and religion are, it would seem, as empty as the Marabar caves. Where there might have been meaning, there is a blank space. Emptiness, nothingness, absence and silence answer any questions we bring to *A Passage to India*.

Any literature which gives readers space to think, in other words any literature which is not crassly didactic, encourages readers to explore the rich offerings of apophatic spirituality. Forster's novel reveals the extraordinariness and strangeness of God, who frustrated characters' expectations, unravelled their beliefs and confronted them with a dark emptiness where enlightenment might be found.

For me, this is the heart of both the literary and theological enterprises. The crux of the difficulty of the literary and theological quest

---

17. Ibid., p. 78.
18. Ibid., p. 145.
19. J.P. Williams, *Seeking the God Beyond: A Beginner's Guide to Christian Apophatic Spirituality* (London: SCM Press, 2018), p.169 (Williams' italics).
20. Lowry, 'Listening for the Echo'.

is to do with the words we use about God, among which one of the most important and (paradoxically) revelatory is the word 'ineffable'. God is beyond description, cannot be defined and is inexpressible. God is essentially and unavoidably beyond words, no matter how much we have to rely on words as primary tools to think about God.

I find that this problem with words is integral to our nature as spiritual beings. It is one of the features that differentiates humans from animals. We are spiritual beings because we are constantly striving to catch a glimpse of God and establish a relationship with God, when direct communication with God is beyond fallen humanity. When we pray, we do not *hear* answers. In my experience, people of sound mind do not usually hear God's voice, either audible externally or in their heads. Rather we encounter a silence – 'a sound of sheer silence' – which speaks to us of One who is absent, but who is also there for us. Such is the strangeness and extraordinariness of the God Forster shows us. Such is the mystery and the wonder of God. And such is what we have to go on in matters of faith.

7

Giving Texts Holy Attention

Close reading began as a mid-twentieth century movement among literary critics which encouraged careful specific study of a text rather than a general impressionistic critique of an author's work. It focussed on the autonomy of a text, paying particular attention to vocabulary, syntax and overall textual structure. It paid less regard to the author's intention when writing, the context in which the text was formed or the culture in which it was being read, but gave priority to the text. The text, so far as it was possible, stood alone. Close reading, as I taught it to A-level students in the 1980s, was so exclusively text-based that it was deemed possible to examine students' literary ability by putting an unseen poem before them and asking them to write a critique. They needed to know nothing of the author or its context. It has its limits as a method of literary criticism. Walter Jackson Bates, a scholar contemporaneous with the movement known as the New Critics, used to mock the concept in his Harvard University lectures with a routine in which he would mutter as he held a book near his face, 'Close reading', 'Closer reading', as he pushed his face into the book and, 'Very close reading', as his nose touched the page so not a word remained legible. His routine was interpreted as a way of ridiculing how close reading's exclusive attention to the text divorces the text from the realities and actualities of life around it, rendering it almost useless. Close reading, Bates was saying, cast the reader adrift without a compass, lost in a sea of sentences.[1]

---

1. Cited in Edmundson, *Why Read?*, pp. 37-38.

I am not using the term 'close reading' in this technical sense in the context of this spirituality of reading. However, the notion of reading a text slowly and carefully, giving full attention to the text as one would in the practice of close reading, contributes to the spiritual benefits reading can bring. We can think of it as a form of 'holy attention', of the type given to sacred texts such as the Talmud, the Quran and the Christian Bible by disciplined and faithful adherents of the Abrahamic faiths. One of the many who bridged two of these faiths was Simone Weil, who was born in 1909 into a Jewish family and became attracted to Christianity through taking retreats at the Benedictine abbey at Solesmes in France. Reciting George Herbert's poem, 'Love bade me welcome', which she had studied so carefully that she had learnt it by heart, she felt that Christ came down and took possession of her. She fled the Nazis and was living in Kent when she died in 1943, still resisting any necessity to be a baptised Christian. Her most famous book is *Waiting for God*, the central idea of which is that prayer begins with attention, in the sense of both waiting and contemplating. Emptying your mind of what is around and within you, you pay close attention to what is in front of you. She argued that, whenever one concentrates on an activity – whether it is learning a new language, trying to balance on a bicycle or conducting an experiment – one is already in an actual contemplative frame of mind.[2] The act of concentration achieves as much. We can add reading a text to the illustrative activities she lists. If I am reading a text with care and concentration, I am exercising what spiritual writers call holy attention.

I can recall reading a reference for a candidate for a senior ecclesiastical role, in which the referee praised the candidate for his ability to read quickly. That did not impress me. For that role, I felt I wanted someone who would read detail with care. I can also recall a minister who read theology by scanning his eye down the centre of the page to get its gist. I felt I wanted a minister who took theology at least a little more seriously. On the other hand, I have been known to encourage students, in an attempt to maximise their use of time, to 'read' text books by studying the index and using it to dip in and out of the book to garner from it whatever they need for the task they have to hand. I suspect that quick scanning and light reading are modern habits, associated with busy and pressured lives within complex societies. As such they could

---

2. See Rowan Williams, *Luminaries: Twenty Lives that Illuminate the Christian Way* (London: SPCK, 2019), p. 128.

Giving Texts Holy Attention

be useful time savers but the incompleteness of such habits results in imprecision and silenced voices.

Close, careful and caring reading of the kind encouraged here encompasses the depth and the range of a text, listens to all the voices, thoughts, arguments and counterarguments within it, and grasps the text's entirety and integrity. It brings to life what lies latent within a book, and it enlivens the empathetic reader with thought, feeling and experience.[3] Taking time with a text rarely disappoints.

In recent years, literary criticism, written for a wider readership than academia alone, has in some instances taken a turn towards close reading of single texts. A notable example is Ian Sansom's publication, *September 1, 1939: A Biography of a Poem* (2019), which dissects W.H. Auden's poem of that title. The poem is an intriguing text because of Auden's own displeasure with it, in contrast with the way it has moved with popular acclaim through the culture of the last 80 years. Although its origins are the day the Second World War broke out when German invaded Poland, it was taken up again on the day a new era of global conflict began when in 2001 Islamist extremists targeted the World Trade Center in New York and the Pentagon in Washington DC with fully loaded passenger jets. 'September 1, 1939' spoke also for '9/11'. Auden more than once disowned the poem. Published first in a periodical in 1939, then in his book of poems, *Another Time*, a year later, he quietly but intentionally dropped it from any of his subsequent publications. He dismissed it as 'trash', a 'damned lie' or 'infected with an incurable dishonesty'. Too late! The poem had already entered the cultural bloodstream of the Anglosphere. This intensely dramatic poem has enjoyed a long public life. Nicholas Jenkins's article in the *Times Literary Supplement*, celebrating the centenary of Auden's birth, records how quickly the poem caught hold:

> The April 6th, 1940 issue of a Communist newsletter called Report to Our Colleagues, probably written by J. Robert Oppenheimer (later to become the 'father' of the Atomic Bomb), attacked Roosevelt, argued against American participation in the European war, and had a quotation from Auden's poem as its epigraph. A year later, the popular British novelist Robert Westerby published

---

3. This point is made by Billington in *Is Literature Healthy?*, p. 135.

Hunger Allows No Choice, a title culled from the eighth stanza of 'September 1, 1939'. Indeed, the poem has been a fruitful source of titles for many other authors: for W. Michael Reisman's *Folded Lies* (1979), an exploration of corruption and bribery, as well as Larry Kramer's play, *The Normal Heart* (1985); for Madelon Powers's *Faces Along the Bar* (1998), a cheery history of saloons, as well as Allen Weinstein's *The Haunted Wood* (1999), a fevered history of Soviet espionage, and, inevitably, Robert G. L. Waite's *The Psychopathic God: Adolf Hitler* (1977). Some phrases from the poem have done double service: David Patterson has published *The Affirming Flame: Religion, Language, Literature* (1988) and Maurice S. Friedman, *The Affirming Flame: A Poetics of Meaning* (1999). From Lyndon Johnson to Dan Quayle, presidents and presidential candidates, or their speechwriters, have similarly ransacked the poem for nuggets of rhetoric.[4]

In the aftermath of 11 September 2001, people were lost for words. The atrocity was quite apocalyptic. The world was never to be the same again. Was all that had been valued before the event now lost forever? How could Western society recover? As often happens when a world falls apart, people sought to come to terms with what had happened by turning to poetry. This is why poetry flourished in the First World War; it is why grandchildren write poems for their grandparents and read them at their funerals; and it is why many in some form of spiritual crisis will turn to a biblical psalm, a great poem of tested worth such as Grey's *Elegy* or a contemporary poem that captures the moment. In 2001, 'September 1, 1939' began a new chapter in its existence. It seemed as if it had been written after, and about, 9/11 despite having preceded it by over 60 years. Adrienne Rich, Paul Muldoon and others read it at impromptu memorials. However, its appeal as a newly meaningful and pertinent text was not only to literary readers but also to the wider public who posted copies of it on their blogs and websites. 'September 1, 1939' was circulated among families and groups of friends by email and, while 'the unmentionable odour of death' still hung in the air, the epigrammatic line 'We must

---

4. Nicholas Jenkins, 'Historical as Munich: Auden at 100: Who Is He Now?', *Times Literary Supplement*, 9 February 2007, pp. 12-15.

love one another or die' was frequently seen on protest placards. The poem rapidly became what Jenkins called 'a peace text', wheeled out once again in 2003 at rallies protesting against the imminent invasion of Iraq, this time citing a different section of the poem:

> I and the public know
> What all schoolchildren learn
> Those to whom evil is done
> Do evil in return.

Although Auden thought the poem dishonest, there is strong evidence to suggest that it begins truthfully. His diary confirms that he did indeed go to a bar called the Dizzy Club on the evening the Second World War began. What troubled him may have been the bad dream he had had in which his lover, Chester Kallman, was unfaithful; it may have been the German invasion of Poland; or it may have been his move to New York from Europe earlier that year for which he had been pilloried in Britain. Over the poem's nine stanzas he worries primarily about Nazism and its threat to democracy and freedom. Auden uses the poem to think through the state of the world and shares his thoughts, as if he is chatting to us as we sit next to him. Perhaps this intimacy about global concerns gives the poem such traction. Perhaps this is what gave it its longevity because it allows the poem to gain and lose meaning, slip in and out of significance, and speak to our age and others. It will forever be reread, rethought and redeployed. You do not have to agree with every aphorism and assertion contained within each of the nine, eleven-line verses – Auden himself did not – to gain from spending time contemplating its lines.

Sansom learns more about himself by reading the poem slowly and writing a personal memoir around it. Readers of his memoir learn much about Sansom too. Time spent with the poem – reading it, thinking about it and writing about it – sets Sansom's personal life into context with his perspective on world affairs. Close reading of the poem locates him within God's world as if reading the poem becomes a form of prayer, although I suspect he himself would not put it that way. As for Sansom, so also for us.

If it is indeed true that reading a poem can be a form of prayer, then we might pay attention to two sonnets separated by 360 years. These are George Herbert's 'Prayer (I)' published in 1633 and Carol Ann Duffy's 'Prayer', published in her collection, *Mean Time*, of 1993.

They bear comparison through slow contemplative reading. We shall soon see that this is not only because they call themselves prayers. The first is Herbert's:

> Prayer the church's banquet, angel's age,
> God's breath in man returning to his birth,
> The soul in paraphrase, heart in pilgrimage,
> The Christian plummet sounding heav'n and earth;
> Engine against th' Almighty, sinner's tow'r,
> Reversed thunder, Christ-side-piercing spear,
> The six-days world transposing in an hour,
> A kind of tune, which all things hear and fear;
> Softness, and peace, and joy, and love, and bliss,
> Exalted manna, gladness of the best,
> Heaven in ordinary, man well drest,
> The milky way, the bird of Paradise,
> Church-bells beyond the stars heard, the soul's blood,
> The land of spices; something understood.

Izaak Walton's biography of Herbert written in 1670 describes his love of music, calling it his 'chiefest recreation', and claims that his twice-weekly visits to Salisbury Cathedral were primarily to hear cathedral music. Herbert was an accomplished lutenist and may have owned several musical instruments. Not only does his musicality translate into the poetry he wrote, but he also makes frequent musical allusions in his verse. He does not keep his hobby out of his work, and this poem is no exception. Music, sound and hearing feature in several ways and, like music in general, the poem is about, and achieves for itself, transfiguration, transposition and transcendence.

Certain features of Herbert's poem are obvious: that it has no finite verb, that it comprises a list of 26 metaphors, and that it reaches no conclusion other than a final image of 'something understood'. The poem works on the basis of gathering a giddying series of images for prayer, whose combined weight, after the break of a semi-colon, falls on this final image. Yet, despite all the weight it carries, Herbert may have intended this image to be open-ended. Some read it as implying something which remains tentative; others find it suggests that the one who prays finds a settled mind. Philip Sheldrake suggested that Herbert chose to use metaphor rather than simile, which is less flexible than metaphor, to resist any unintended implication in the sonnet that prayer can be defined. Herbert, it seems, wanted to achieve the sense that prayer is a mysterious process by which we touch the ultimate mystery. The metaphors of 'Prayer (I)', behaving as all metaphors do, swing between heaven and earth, between time and eternity, in the way that prayer bridges these two realms.[5]

Some of the images reverse the expected norms, giving the impression that Herbert is wrestling with the limits of language to express the extraordinariness and peculiarity of prayer as a practice. A plummet that reaches up to plumb the height of heaven, manna which is lifted up rather than dropped to earth and 'reversed thunder' in their upside-downness are almost nonsensical. Some aspects of prayer are equally illogical.

The sonnet's opening couplet employs images which bring us at the outset of the poem straight to the central paradox of prayer: it is both communal and intensely private. As the 'Church's banquet', a phrase reminding us of the Eucharist, a foretaste of the heavenly banquet, prayer is both our spiritual food and a shared common experience. An individual's prayer is pooled with those of others and becomes the Church's. Yet it remains as personal as God's breath in us, the source of life coursing through our veins, our lifeblood. Nothing can be more intimate than the breath within our lungs and the blood flowing through our bodies, yet this personal, mortal intimacy is as timeless as the angels. As if to stress the importance of this to Herbert, the sonnet will return to this in the penultimate line when it calls prayer the 'soul's blood'. Despite this intimacy between the one who prays and prayer, prayer transcends human limits and takes us from the temporal world into the time of angels; prayer is 'angel's age'.

The work of a poet is to exploit the potential of language. At times this may mean paraphrasing text to expand its meaning, exploring the height, breadth and depth of its words. I think this is what lies behind the image of 'the soul in paraphrase': prayer expands the soul to its full potential even to the extent of bringing us into the presence of God as the source of life. It is equally true that prayer can be the most complete expression of our deepest selves. If we want to employ spatial metaphors, we might say that prayer lifts up what is deep down within ourselves to God, pulling the heart ever onwards on its pilgrimage through the wilderness of earth towards the fullness of eternity and

---

5. Philip Sheldrake, ed., *Heaven in Ordinary: George Herbert and His Writings* (Norwich: Canterbury Press, 2009), p. 148.

the glory of the heavenly city (if you will allow me to introduce to Herbert's already heavily image-laden conversation yet more familiar images). Prayer is the engine powering the journey.

The complexity of the human pilgrimage – no life journey is as straight as a Roman road across a plain – comes to the fore among Herbert's free-flowing torrent of images in lines that often trouble me and make me pause to think about them more. In what way, I ask, is prayer an 'Engine against th' Almighty, sinner's tow'r / Reversed thunder, Christ-side-splitting spear'? These images are belligerent, pugilistic images of prayer, bombarding God in the way that a medieval siege engine is mounted against the walls of a city, the citizens of which seek to defend themselves and resist the advances of marauders. Does God defend Godself and close God's ears to the supplicants so firmly that they have to attack to gain admission? 'Sinner's tow'r' implies that the one who prays must be strong, resilient and persevering to be heard, and the voice of prayer needs to be as loud and insistent as thunder pealing towards the skies, reversing its usual earthward trajectory. Prayer, it seems, needs to be so insistent that, like the soldier's spear thrust into the crucified Jesus, the final wound on his battered body to make sure he was dead, it pierces God's side. By the way, in another of his poems, 'The Bag', Herbert has Christ invite supplicants to write their prayers and place them into this wound so that they are close to God's heart: the dying Christ, indicating the wound in his side, says, 'Look, you may put it very neare my heart'. In 'Prayer (I)' the image may, therefore, not be quite as violent as it first seems. Nonetheless, the cumulative effect of the images in this couplet is of prayer as combat, appropriate for lives that are a struggle, pilgrimages through hostile land and tortured spiritualities. For Herbert, and for others, battling with God is not unusual.

On other occasions, though, prayer is as transformative and consoling as the sweetest music, transposing the workaday world into another key, making a sabbath of a working day and providing a heavenly rest for the labouring soul. Prayer transforms the quotidian world of the six-day working week into a tune heard by all and bringing all into the awful presence of God (interpreting 'fear' to mean awe, wonder and reverence). Sheldrake tells us that in Herbert's day an 'ordinary' was either the regular menu of cheap food served in a tavern or the rough part of the inn where such food was served,[6]

---

6. Ibid., p. 159.

so the phrase 'heaven in ordinary' reverses the sense of the previous section: not only does prayer transpose the ordinary into sacredness, but conversely, through the practice of prayer, God is found among the ordinary things of life. This notion of the mundane world being transfigured by divine glory is further described through two images of the natural world of contrasting scales – the galactic Milky Way and the detailed beauty of a bird of paradise. Prayer is a thing of great majesty and of intricate beauty.

Despite the soberness of the sonnet's subject, joy characterises much of it. John Drury suggests Herbert achieves this by appealing to each of the senses, as well as to the intellect: to taste through 'the Church's banquet'; to sight through 'the bird of paradise' and the 'milky way'; to hearing through thunder 'a kind of tune' and 'church-bells beyond the stars heard'; to touch through 'softness'; to smell through 'land of spices'; then finally, to the mind in 'something understood'.[7] None of this reduces the overall sense in the poem that prayer is a complex mixture of paradoxes, both a struggle and a joy, both a battle with God and an easing into the presence of God. Over all, the poem leaves me asking whether prayer is primarily sensual or intellectual. Is it a matter of feeling or mental concentration? However, it is probably unfair to express these as a binary question!

St Paul wrote about the difficulties of prayer in his letter to the Romans. It was no easier for him than it was for George Herbert. When Paul did not know the words to use, he remarked, 'We do not know how to pray as we ought, but that very Spirit intercedes with sighs too deep for words'.[8] Carol Ann Duffy's poem also begins when prayer is difficult, when the words will not come, and, like Herbert's sonnet, (and, indeed, most of Charles Wesley's hymns) it also ends in heaven, at the ends of the earth. I suspect this is happenstance rather than intention. The final word in the poem is 'Finisterre', referring to part of the shipping forecast, a sea area now known as Fitzroy. Finisterre means 'end of the world,' being derived from *finis terrae*. We might read this as implying that the end goal of prayer is a point of arrival, and that prayer is a repeated call.

As an introduction to the work of the former poet laureate, Carol Ann Duffy's 'Prayer' features on many school and college curricula

---

7. John Drury, *Music at Midnight: The Life and Poetry of George Herbert* (London: Allen Lane, 2013), p. 337.

8. Romans 8:26 (NRSV).

so it is widely known. In the form of a sonnet, it comprises three quatrains, rhyming *abab, cdcd, efef,* followed by a couplet which repeats the *aa* rhyme of the first stanza. The *aa* rhyme at the beginning of the poem is 'prayer' and 'stare', repeated in the concluding couplet's rhyme of 'prayer' and 'Finisterre' reinforcing the sense that the poem ends where it began. The end takes us back to the beginning; and our struggle with prayer takes us, if not to the gates of heaven, at least to the end of the earth, Finisterre.

The first and second stanzas of Duffy's 'Prayer' are paired: the first tells of some days when we cannot find the words to pray while the second tells of some nights when we find ourselves without faith. In the first, 'when we cannot pray' prayer 'utters itself'; one's inability to pray is answered with a sudden gift. A woman who has, until now, held her head in her hand in despair lifts her gaze and, in a curious mixture of sight and hearing 'stare[s] / at the minims sung by a tree'. The natural world has responded to her despair. In the second stanza, a man hearing the distant sound of a train is transported to the happier time of his childhood. By paying attention to the world around him, he 'hear[s] his youth' in the prayer-like throb of the engine, whether steam or diesel, and in the wheel's chatter along the tracks, what the poet calls the 'Latin chanting' of the train. These 'prayers' are given, rather than uttered by the one trying to pray; they come as a gift from what this woman and man see or hear around them, in one case, in the natural world and, in the other case, in the constructed world. These gifts lift their spirits.

The third stanza begins with a bidding: evoking the *Ave Maria*, 'Pray for us sinners, now, and at the hour of our death', the poet, associating herself with the woman and man to whom she has referred, now directly addresses the reader and asks that we pray for all of them: 'Pray for us'. We are invited to pray for all who despairingly hold their heads in their hands and all who, numbed by adverse experience, 'stand stock-still'. In short, we are invited to pray for all who suffer. The response to the invitation to pray, and to prayer itself, is consolation through the acknowledgement of suffering. The distant sounds of piano practice reaching across a Midlands town and of a child being called in from playing outside as night falls are heard either as prayer itself or as answer to prayer. Through them, loss is recognised and 'named' and these sympathetic sounds are the beginning of consolation and support. Memory of better times encourages the soul in harder times. These simple things have been the beginning of remedy.

In the sonnet's concluding couplet, whatever else is going on – 'darkness outside' and pain, loneliness, loss 'inside' – we learn that the interior voice of prayer is never silent. The radio's prayer is the shipping forecast, whose regularity and dependability reassure not only those at sea but many a listener tossing and turning in their beds at night. The forecaster's chanting of the sea areas, like a daily litany, can bring peace to the restless and calm to the stressed. The numinous is in the everyday.

Duffy's 'Prayer' is about the repetitiveness of prayer, the routine and ritual of prayer, the monotony of prayer. This theme is emphasised in the way the sonnet keeps to iambic pentameter throughout, giving the poem itself a strong rhythm of persistent repetition. When I was a child, my parents taught me to pray by using the same prayer each night. They were Methodists so it should be no surprise that they taught me to pray by learning by heart, and reciting nightly, the first verse of a Charles Wesley hymn:

> Gentle Jesus, meek and mild,
> Look upon a little child,
> Pity my simplicity,
> Suffer me to come to thee.

After this, I was invited to add petitions that God might bless Mummy and Daddy, my grandparents and anyone else I loved. To conclude, I should look beyond my immediate world and ask God to bless all the children of the world. Night by night it never changed. I was learning that prayer had a format, and this continues in my experience of what we call an 'order' of prayer, whether this is a daily office, such as that read by a priest, the structure of a collect, or the discipline of a chosen prayer time. Nonconformist prayer, which can seem over-familiar and casually conversational, is also structured and disciplined. Rarely is it an entirely free-flowing stream of consciousness. Careful observers of charismatic prayer meetings should be able to detect structure and order in what they hear there, too. It is less obvious but no less real than in the written liturgies of those denominations favouring formality. Indeed, in the prayer meetings that followed public worship in the Methodist chapel I attended as a teenager, there was something disappointingly predictable about who would pray and what they would pray. The Latin chanting Duffy refers to is not as far removed from Nonconformist and Pentecostal prayer as we might first think.

In the midst of the pandemic of 2020, Jarel Robinson-Brown wrote movingly about the monotony of prayer in the May edition of 'Signs of the Times', a leaflet produced by Modern Church, an organisation devoted to the promotion of liberal theology in Britain. Robinson-Brown spoke of praying 'Compline' while Covid-19 ravaged the world. Each night of his life as a Benedictine Oblate he prayed through Psalm 91: 'You will not fear the terror of the night, nor the arrow that flies by day, nor the plague that prowls in the darkness, nor the scourge that lays waste at noon. A thousand may fall at your side, ten thousand at your right' (verses five to seven). He asked what it meant to pray those words as thousands died and thousands more were kept alive on ventilators each day. He knows that he owes his faith almost entirely to his grandmother and he observes that, had she not died when she did, she, as an older black woman, would likely not have lived long in 2020. He asks, 'What does it mean to fall to one's knees in prayer in a world which feels as though it has fallen apart and in which prayer seems a redundant action? What does it mean to fall to one's knees in prayer in a world in which God appears to have fallen silent?'[9] Wrestling with the task of praying as he ought, he recalls that his grandmother used to say, 'We're coming from afar.' Until now he did not understand what she meant. Now he knows she meant that, regardless of where we are, we are not the first to stand here and we shall not be the last. The discipline of nightly prayer links him with all who have prayed in that way across the centuries and with all who will take up the discipline in future. The contexts of those prayers of the past and future are various: monks, nuns, martyrs and pilgrims have prayed, and will pray again, the same prayer in war and peace, poverty and prosperity, famine and plenty, persecution and plague, pouring out what Robinson-Brown calls 'the incompetence of my prayer'. This encouraged him to persist in the monotony of prayer each night, never knowing if, how or when the pandemic he was praying through would come to an end. I find that Robinson-Brown's testimony establishes the value of keeping to a routine in prayer,

---

9. Jarel Robinson-Brown, 'Living in the Monotony of Prayer', Modern Church website. Available online at: https://modernchurch.org.uk/jarel-robinson-brown-living-in-the-monotony-of-prayer (accessed 13 July 2024).

being part of a tradition of prayer and the vital role of routine in a healthy spiritual life.

In my view, Herbert's and Duffy's sonnets on prayer have merited being discussed in parallel. Reading one after the other prompts me to ask which image of prayer makes most sense in our experience of modern life – wrestling as an engine against the Almighty or a monotonous routine which gives the occasional glimpse of knowledge and insight?

When considered together like this, Herbert's 'Prayer (I)' and Duffy's 'Prayer' remind me, in their different ways, of James Montgomery's 'Prayer is the soul's sincere desire, uttered or unexpressed', a hymn which often punctuated the prayer meetings I attended in the church of my teenage years. Montgomery was a Moravian hymn writer and poet, remembered more for the few hymns of his that are still sung than for his more-or-less unread poetry. Like Herbert's sonnet, each verse of the hymn introduces a fresh image for prayer and, like Duffy's 'Prayer', it describes prayer's ability to lift us to the ends of the earth and the gate of heaven despite, or because of, its ordinariness and repetition. As in both sonnets, the hymn teaches us that we do not stand alone in prayer. We pray with the communion of saints:

> Prayer is the soul's sincere desire,
> uttered or unexpressed;
> the motion of a hidden fire
> that trembles in the breast.
>
> Prayer is the burden of a sigh,
> the falling of a tear,
> the upward glancing of an eye
> when none but God is near.
>
> Prayer is the simplest form of speech
> that infant lips can try,
> prayer the sublimest strains that reach
> the Majesty on high.
>
> Prayer is the Christian's vital breath,
> the Christian's native air,
> his watchword at the gates of death:
> he enters heaven with prayer.

> Prayer is the contrite sinner's voice,
> returning from his ways;
> while angels in their songs rejoice,
> and cry, 'Behold, he prays!'
>
> The saints in prayer appear as one,
> in word and deed and mind;
> while with the Father and the Son
> sweet fellowship they find.
>
> O Thou by whom we come to God,
> the Life, the Truth, the Way,
> the path of prayer thyself hast trod:
> Lord, teach us how to pray!

In an unguarded moment I once asked a modern hymnwriter whether he also wrote poetry. I could have asked the question less brusquely, but I persist in the view that the skills required of a hymnwriter differ from, though they are related to, those of a poet. I feel sure, therefore, that, although Montgomery wrote this hymn for singing, he brought his skills as a poet to the text in such a way that, like Herbert's and Duffy's sonnets, it can be meditated upon, verse by verse, as a spiritual exercise.

Such close reading is, in my view, none other than holy attention. In 2016 David Marno published a book which could be placed alongside Sansom's, although it is much less personal and more academic in nature. It is a close reading of John Donne's sonnet, 'Death Be Not Proud',[10] used to bolster Marno's argument that time-honoured traditions of attentiveness as ways of knowing God are related to the modern practices of close reading. He demonstrates that Donne's poem was written in the context of devotional practices, in which language is used to cultivate attentiveness. The poem is akin to prayer. His argument, demonstrated through Donne's poem, could serve as a conclusion to my discussion of Auden, Herbert and Duffy.

To aid understanding of the full extent of Marno's argument, I need to take you back to Nicolas Malebranche, French theologian and Cartesian philosopher of the second half of the seventeenth

---

10. David Marno, *Death Be Not Proud: The Art of Holy Attention* (Chicago: University of Chicago Press, 2016).

Giving Texts Holy Attention

century, who argued that thinking is like prayer on the basis that the outcome of each is beyond our control. He equated the philosopher's use of rational thought in pursuit of truth with the believer's prayer in its quest for communion with God. My work on this spirituality of reading leads me to the opinion that thinking is like prayer in more ways than this. Each can be deliberate in that I can think through a problem and I can set aside time and space to kneel in prayer, and each can be involuntary in that I might be struck by a random thought and a petition to God might spring to my mind uninvited. Malebranche's insight was to suggest that attentiveness is, in Marno's words, 'the cultivation of a passive disposition, a solicitous waiting for a conversation to happen'.[11] Intentional stilling of the mind prepares the ground for either thought or prayer; and Malebranche observed that to think better we first must learn how to pray better.

Marno implies that the key to better prayer is greater attentiveness. In contemporary Nonconformist churches in Britain a distinction is often made between attenders and members. Those who are church attenders are usually regarded as slightly less committed to church than those who participate as church members. This is because we tend to see attending as a passive activity. However, 'attend' comes to the English language, by way of French for waiting, from the Latin *attendere* meaning stretching towards. Its primary meaning, therefore, is to direct one's faculties towards something or someone; 'attending' is 'paying attention'. If we think of attention in this more active mode, we must ask what kind of attention we should pay to the *words* of a prayer and what kind of attention we should give to the addressee, by which I mean whatever lies *beyond* the prayer. The traditional postures of prayer may be pertinent at this point. We teach children to put their hands together in prayer to discourage fidgeting and the common folding together of our hands in prayer is a mark of concentration. However, the original gesture for Christian prayer was to stand with raised, outstretched arms as a sign of offering and openness to God. Both the original and the now-common postures include a sense of concentrated waiting.

In Donne's day many devotional handbooks noted how hard it was to sustain concentration when praying and they advised on ways to get rid of all distractions. At the funeral of Sir William Cokayne on 12 December 1626, Donne preached a sermon and spoke of 'the

---

11. Ibid., p. 1.

manifold weaknesses of the strongest devotions in time of prayer'. He might throw himself down to pray in his room yet allow the buzzing of a fly, the rattle of a coach or the whining of a door to disturb his prayer. He continued, 'A memory of yesterdays pleasure, a feare of tomorrows dangers, a straw under my knee, a noise in mine eare, a light in mine eye, an any thing, a nothing, a fancy, a Chimera in my braine, troubles me in my prayer.'[12] He thought of this as a natural aspect of the fallen human condition and, if he ever managed attentiveness, he saw it as a minor miracle resulting from divine action: we can be attentive because in a moment of prayer God brings together our fractured and splintered selves. Aquinas asked whether attention is necessary to prayer directly and offered three answers: prayer can only be 'in spirit' if it is attentive; prayer can only be an ascent to God if it is attentive; and prayer is sinful if the mind wanders. Yet he gives the distracted devotee a glimmer of compensation when he observes that fallen humanity is simply not capable of maintaining the level of concentration required for effective prayer. In other words, attentiveness is necessary, but it is not possible. What a bind! This, and Donne's struggle to concentrate and avoid distraction when praying, raises a question about the nature of prayer: to what extent is prayer a technique and to what extent is it an expression of religious feeling? Or, to express that question differently, to what extent is prayer something *we* achieve through the practice of holy attention, and to what extent is it something God achieves in and for us as an act of grace? Do we consciously pray or does prayer come to us? These questions take us back to Paul's struggle in Romans: 'We do not know how to pray as we ought, but that very Spirit intercedes with sighs too deep for words.'

It is like falling asleep, says Marno. He noted that Renaissance poetry called the gift of sleep 'heavy grace' because the process of falling asleep is neither active nor passive. Think of what you do – or what happens to you – nightly, whether it is easy or not. Strictly speaking going to sleep is not an action because one is not asleep until sleep has overcome or subdued one. On the other hand, especially if sleep often evades you, those trying to sleep often *do* things to prepare for sleep. We turn off all electronic devices, we read a book, we close the curtains and switch off the light. Marno points out that some of

---

12. Theodore Gill, ed., *The Sermons of John Donne* (New York, NY: Meridian Books, 1958), pp. 181-82.

these actions are mimetic in that we imitate our sleeping selves by closing our eyes, lying down and breathing more calmly and deeply. The sleep that comes is, in part, a result of these actions and, in part, as a gift. Similarly, in Malebranche's philosophy of prayer, active attentiveness seeking grace makes space for grace to come. Such holy attention can be either highly ritualised or relatively casual.

It has long been thought that Donne wrote many of the poems we know as his Holy Sonnets when he was agonising over his decision to take holy orders and that they were influenced by the spiritual exercises of the Ignatian tradition. Indeed, they may be themselves meditations to help Donne reach a decision about his vocation.[13]

The goal of holy attention is twofold: one to achieve a state of thankfulness, the other to know God. Thus, as Marno says, 'Holy attention in the sense of a perfectly undistracted, intransitive attention is a feature of *pure* prayer.'[14] Yet Augustine in his *Confessions* admitted that his life was a distraction, primarily a distraction from praise of God. My argument for the practice of close reading as a spiritual exercise is that giving holy attention to a poem brings us into a prayerful condition, what Marno calls 'poems that pray, prayers that think, and thinking that attends'.[15]

This chapter has shown three features of a spirituality of close reading. These are, first, that the reward received for concentrated reading of a text is to achieve deeper, undistracted communion with God in prayer. The second feature is that the beginning of this deep communion lies in the process of waiting. The more attentive one is, the 'better' one prays – by 'better' I mean 'more intimate' because God's spirit prays through us, which is to say that the prayer is inspired. God repays any discipline or effort involved on the part of the person at prayer. The third feature is one of correlation between thought and prayer. This reasserts Malebranche's notion that thinking is like praying. In short, this chapter has been about concentrating and praying, waiting and praying, thinking and praying.

---

13. Marno, *Death Be Not Proud*, p. 20.
14. Ibid., p. 112 (Marno's italics).
15. Ibid., p. 38.

8

The Beauty of Books

Percy Dearmer, the early twentieth-century hymn writer who collaborated with the composers Ralph Vaughan Williams and Martin Shaw to produce *Songs of Praise* (1925) as a hymnbook for use in schools, wrote a hymn whose refrain was 'God is good! God is truth! God is beauty! Praise him!' The last of these proclamations, that God is beauty, is what Hans Urs von Balthasar called God's most neglected attribute. It is true that, there is much less discussion of God as beauty than there is of God as either goodness or truth. I suspect this may be because the relationship between God and beauty is problematic.

Some years ago, Leonard Nimoy, the actor most famous for playing the part of Spock in the television series *Star Trek*, published a collection of his photographs under the title *Shekhina* (2002). Nimoy was both Jewish and fervently atheist. This collection of photographs is intended to depict the feminine side of the divine nature, and we might recall that *shekhinah* is the Hebrew word for the glory or radiance of God's presence. The collection was received with mixed reactions of surprise and shock because many of the photographs featured semi-nude female models wearing tallit and tefillin, normally worn by Jewish men when praying. The monochrome cover photograph, the one with which I am most familiar, shows a woman whose breast is covered by no more than a diaphanous robe as she rises above a stretch of water with the straps of a tefillin on one arm. When I first saw this, frankly beautiful, photograph I was given its title as 'God'. Many of us might ask how Nimoy's photograph of a beautiful woman depicts God.

The problems with beauty are, first, that it is subjective and, second, that tastes change. For instance, when I was younger, art deco was unfashionable but now the genre has become popular once more and I would have to pay premium prices for some art deco furniture. Similarly, my personal preferences also change: I am now much more likely to appreciate Muslim ceramics than when I felt that pattern in art was less important than naturalistic realism. We cannot escape the reality that there are various ways to appreciate and understand beauty. The classical western conception of beauty is one of order and proportion, perspective and harmony, while the Japanese way has an aesthetic of imperfection. Consequently, a broken vase repaired with gold is regarded as more beautiful than when it was in its original perfect condition. The Yoruba of Nigeria have a yet different understanding of beauty; for them, beauty is a matter of particularity, a matter of what differentiates one thing from everything else. This variety of views about what is beautiful reminds me of my time as chaplain to the Stuart Crystal factory in the early 1980s. The glassblowers and cutters prided themselves, quite rightly, on their expert mouth-blown, hand-cut product. No one glass was exactly the same as another. Each had the mark of its craftworkers. However, this individuality and particularity was challenged at the time by the growing Asian market for British cut glass. This new market wanted a perfect match within a set of glasses, something that could only be achieved if the product was machine-blown and cut by machine. No definitive answer to the question: 'Which is more beautiful – the perfect machine-made or the individualistic handcrafted glass?' could ever be reached to the satisfaction of everyone.

Richard Harries suggests that beauty is the appreciation of form. This, too, is a problematic word. Form has more than twenty definitions and Angela Leighton finds it a term that is 'thick with possible echoes and conflicting references'[1] and yet it is a term we cannot avoid in the appreciation and critique of literature. Every work of art has form of one kind or another. Poetry, for instance, uses metre, rhythm and rhyme to shape poems. Forms can change and new forms can emerge, as when Wilfred Owen made use of half-rhymes, assonance and internal rhyming and when Gerard Manley Hopkins developed sprung rhythm, instress and inscape. Harries stressed

---

1. Angela Leighton, *On Form: Poetry, Aestheticism, and the Legacy of a Word* (Oxford: Oxford University Press, 2007), p. 2.

that form is inescapable in art: it is what 'distinguishes a painting from a splurge of paint, music from a cacophony of sound, a novel or play from a rambling anecdote'.[2] Yet we cannot be precise about this: an artist might splash and flick badly aimed paint on a canvas, a composer could create an ear-jarring clash of noise, and a novelist could write a rambling anecdote within a novel.

Some art is capable of appealing to every culture and age – the Taj Mahal seems to disappoint no one, whilst some might be underwhelmed by the Mona Lisa – but most art appreciation seems to be conditioned by our culture, our time and our education. Chinese opera, Japanese Noh theatre and some medieval English literature are currently outside the limits of my definition of beauty because I do not know enough about them to understand them, but this could change. Tastes change from age to age and this makes me ask whether beauty can ever be objective. Whilst Harries is correct to assert that whatever is truly beautiful will in time be universally recognised as such, it must also be true that it is both idiotic and a form of cultural arrogance either to disdain what someone else regards as beautiful or to seek to tell others that they must agree that what I regard as beautiful is indeed so. Proverbs become proverbs because they carry some truth, so we should accept the truth of the adage that beauty is in the eye of the beholder.

Any pleasure we might take in beauty is an individual personal response to what we see, but Paul Guyer argued that what we see and take pleasure in is the form of the object. We do not necessarily respond to any matter or content the object has.[3] However, Leighton suggests that, in the case of literature, the form we perceive may be one of three things: either the shape of the text on the page (or the structure of a novel spread over many pages), the shape of the sounds the text makes in the air when it is recited or read aloud, or the matter of which the text speaks. She seems to prefer not to separate form from content. In a similar vein, Roland Barthes, the great French literary theorist, suggests that form acts as a go-between which interrupts the link between a thing and its name. In other words, the form of a text breaks the norms of representation and obstructs the seamlessness of links between the text on the page and whatever the

---

2. Richard Harries, *Art and the Beauty of God: A Christian Understanding* (London: Mowbray, 1993), p. 22.
3. Quoted in Leighton, *On Form*, p. 5.

text signifies. Any otherwise obvious and brisk link between signifier and signified is, at least, delayed and possibly broken by an unusual or unexpected form of a text, and this gives readers pause for thought and may, indeed, make them reroute their thinking quite radically.[4] Barthes, therefore, suggests that form stops us in the tracks of our thought processes and inserts itself into that moment of stillness. Thus, giving attention to the form of a text has again become an important aspect of critical thinking. It gives a work its identifying mark and its structural footprint, without which art would lack its distinguishing characteristic.

I feel that it is important to emphasise that form is not a matter of correct technique, like the counting of syllables in iambic pentameter or making consistent rhyme schemes within a stanza. Rather, it is what Leighton simply called a 'force of creativity generally'.[5] This results in form being both an ill-defined and a powerful critical concept. To consider the form of a piece is not to consider questions of verse form or metre, but to appreciate the aesthetics of a piece and to consider how the form serves the meaning and the art. No work of art can be formless. Many works of art may not conform with pre-existing conventions; some may shatter those conventions. Some literary texts may follow strict conventions; others may play with those conventions. I can recall that, as a schoolboy studying for A-level English, I struggled with the eighteenth-century poets we were expected to study. It seemed to me that some of these poets were too intent on mimicking ancient poetic forms such as Pindaric odes, and were so slavish in their efforts to replicate them in eighteenth-century style that, to my naïve mind, all freedom and joy in the art was lost. I later realised that I was quite wrong in my youthful impressions. Rather it is true that poets throughout the ages have found freedom of expression within the seemingly unyielding parameters of the sonnet form and many other forms. No poem is formless; every poem is its own form; every poem has its own shape and pattern, and these serve the poem's purpose and its aesthetic. The art of the poem is art for art's sake. Remembering that beauty is not always pretty, in that the beauty of art can be ugly, horrifying and eccentric, we should note that what matters is not that the beautiful thing is attractive, but that the beautiful thing is related to truth. If we accept this definition of

---

4. Ibid., pp. 20-21.
5. Ibid., p. 23.

what is beauty in art, including literature, it should be plain to see that the beauty of a text can indeed speak of the beauty of God, and bring us closer to God.

To attempt to show this potential to you, I feel that the best place to turn is the poem that may already have come to your mind as you read this chapter, namely John Keats's *Ode on a Grecian Urn* (1819), whose final couplet claims:

> Beauty is truth, truth beauty, – that is all
> Ye know on earth, and all ye need to know.

This statement seems conclusive, as if Keats is saying there is nothing more to say on the matter. In her discussion of this poem, Angela Leighton states that 'Beautiful and useless, the urn exists in an empty space … without contest, history, origin or destination.'[6] It is an empty container that remembers a former use and a lost content. Now no longer used for its original purpose, it is simply there, and the poem both gives the urn its shape and takes its shape. Like art for art's sake, the urn is there for its own sake only. For this reason, Leighton suggests that the syllogism in inverted commas in the poem's penultimate line does not solve a problem but makes us aware of the problem: 'Beauty is truth, truth beauty,' does not assert a conclusion, but reveals a crack, a break, a gap between truth and beauty which we see in the poem in the form of a comma separating the repeated word 'truth'. We hear this join when we read the line. In short, Keats seems to have known and to be saying that a thing of beauty is related to the truth, that a thing of beauty can say something important about the world, human existence and ultimate meaning, but he also seems to be asserting that there is no perfect match between beauty and truth.[7]

In contrast, the golden bowl, in Henry James's 1904 novel, *The Golden Bowl*, tells a different story to that told by Keats's Grecian urn. Unlike the urn, which we assume to be flawless, James's bowl is broken. The bowl in the antique shop is worth nothing because the crystal glass under the gold veneer is cracked. The veneer hides the flaws; any beauty in the bowl is only skin deep. When the bowl is hurled to the floor and broken into three pieces, Maggie says to her unfaithful husband, 'Its having come apart makes an unfortunate

---

6. Ibid., p. 40.
7. Ibid., p. 41.

difference for its beauty, its artistic value, but none for anything else. Its other value is still the same – I mean that of its having given me so much of the truth of you.'[8] Even so, Maggie holds the broken pieces in her cupped hands and it is remarked that the bowl might still quite beautifully have passed for uninjured. Here James is widening the gap between truth and beauty that Keats implied, and seems to be saying that beauty might survive a break with truth value, moral value and monetary value.[9] Divorced from truth, beauty survives alone. The reason for this is that beauty is more to do with form than with what it might mean.

A recently published discussion of beauty suggests that beauty is the answer to what its author calls 'the Question'.[10] Nick Riggle has had this question lodged in his mind since adolescence: because we did not ask to be born, why should we embrace life? First-time fatherhood has brought this question to the fore once again for Riggle. By exploring the life-affirming clichés of popular culture – such as 'Seize the day', 'You only live once', 'Live in the moment' – he concludes that beauty is the reason we should be glad to be alive. If we live actively and attentively, if we live fully and enthusiastically, we live in a manner which is open to appreciate beauty wherever and whenever it is encountered. This encounter with beauty calls forth from within us a desire to share beauty, to replicate beauty and to find self-expression in beauty. This gives Riggle a reason to enjoy being alive, and he argues that we can all enjoy life because we can appreciate whatever is beautiful. When the philosopher Kieran Setiya reviewed Riggle's book, he agreed with the author that beauty's value is not just ameliorative, in that it solves a problem or meets a need so that we would rather not be without it, but also that it has an existential value because it makes it 'positively good to be alive'.[11] However, there are other things, he said, that can make us glad to be alive, so beauty is not the only answer to Riggle's 'Big Question' but it is a good one. Beauty renders life not just worth living, but worth savouring.

---

8. Quoted in ibid., p. 43.
9. Ibid., p. 43.
10. Nick Riggle, *This Beauty: A Philosophy of Being Alive* (London: Hachette, 2022).
11. Kieran Setiya, 'The Line of Beauty: Why We're Glad to Be Alive', *Times Literary Supplement*, 18 November 2022, p. 29.

In one of the last sermons I preached in my active ministry, I explored two themes that I feel are closely related: home and paradise. The sermon was inspired by the words given to Jesus in the fourth Gospel that he is going to his Father's house to prepare a place for us, as well as by Paul's claim in the letter to the Philippians that our citizenship is in heaven. Using insights from religious philosophies other than Christianity as well as biblical insights, the sermon explored the idea that a longing for home or a search for paradise is common to all human experience. It is present in all religious faiths and in all artistic disciplines. All people look for a place to call home, somewhere they feel they belong. In some cases this takes the form of a longing for a better place than the world we inhabit now. As towards the end of John Milton's *Paradise Lost*, Adam and Eve were commissioned to find a happier and better paradise than the Eden from which they have been banished, so there is in many people a thirst for a better place which inspires a spiritual quest for paradise. The sense of incompleteness we feel in our transient existence prompts discontent with mundane existence and a yearning for something greater and better. This often leads to taking recourse to story because, as the novelist Elif Shafak said in *Three Daughters of Eve*, when we live in limbo between 'what was' and the 'not yet', storyland is our only motherland.[12] When we see beauty around us in this life, this draws us to seek the hidden beauty that is beyond this world. This search for a lost Eden fuels our appreciation of beauty, and our experiences of beauty arouse a yearning for God and a longing for communion with God's beauty. All this because it is in the nature of a finite creature to reach towards the infinite. Even though paradise is beyond our grasp the very fact that we know it is beyond our grasp is an essential part of our awareness of our finitude and incompleteness. This is very much what makes us spiritual beings.

There is a strong biblical tradition that order is an important aspect of God's beauty. The first Genesis account of creation depicted God speaking creation into order. By giving each part of creation its proper name, God ordered the world into being: day and night first, sky and earth, the oceans and dry land and so on until the final ordering distinguished the holy day of rest from working days. Upheaval and chaos fall upon us whenever this order is disrupted, for example, when flood waters encroach on the land and when stormy

---

12. Elif Shafak, *Three Daughters of Eve* (New York, NY: Bloomsbury, 2016).

seas threaten to upturn boats on Galilee, or at a personal level when our failure to observe a sabbath harms our mental wellbeing. Both the prophets and wisdom literature repeated the importance of God's order: God is said to have ordered all things by measure, number and weight.[13] What follows this way of looking at the creativity of God is to see that human beings, who are made in God's image, also have the capacity to be similarly creative. We, too, can put things in order and create beauty. Richard Harries made the same point: 'artists of every kind share in the work of the divine artist by giving form to recalcitrant matter. They make music of inchoate sounds and speech of incoherent babble. They give shape to the shapeless and in so doing reflect the work of eternal wisdom.'[14] This is why the artist Michelangelo believed that all earthly beauty and anything beautiful made by a human being originated in God, saying of his own work that whatever he carved from a block of marble began with a concept in his mind that could only have begun in God's mind. Earthly beauty was inspired by, and reflected, divine beauty.

William Blake encapsulated something of this connection between form and beauty in his *Songs of Innocence* and *Songs of Experience* of, respectively, 1789 and 1794. Blake imagined these as companion texts showing what he called 'the two contrary states of the human soul', uncorrupted and experienced. The poems in each volume are not directly matched with companion pieces in the other volume, but there are several points of correlation. 'The Lamb', the fourth poem in *Songs of Innocence*, is, for instance, related in some ways with 'The Tyger' in the *Songs of Experience*, that relationship being made specific in the penultimate stanza when the poet refers back to the earlier poem. The former poem asks, 'Little Lamb who made thee?', while the latter asks the tiger, 'What immortal hand or eye could frame thy fearful symmetry?' 'The Lamb', by modern standards, is twee. The lamb's delightful clothing, 'softest clothing wooly bright', and its 'tender voice, / Making all the vales rejoice' are what prompt Blake to ask whether the creature is aware who made it. However, when he looks at a tiger he must ask, 'Did he who made the Lamb make thee?' This creature is of a different order altogether. The tiger's power and majesty strike awe and wonder in the onlooker who, at first, asks who could create such a beast but who, after further examination of

---

13. Wisdom 11:20.
14. Harries, *Art and the Beauty of God*, p. 102.

his subject, asks who would *dare* to create such a beast. The tiger's 'fearful symmetry' that inspired Blake to write was not pretty in the way a lamb can be attractive but it is indubitably a form of beauty. It is beauty that inspired Blake; and his illuminated manuscript of the poem is beautiful, too. 'The Tyger' is literary beauty imitating divine beauty.

When we read a novel, what bearing do these notions of beauty, form, order and design have on any spiritual benefit we derive from reading the novel?

* * *

Mark Edmundson's book, *Why Read?*, was a response to the decline of religion as an influence on many sections of society and it argued that, in the absence of religion, literature 'is *the* major cultural source of vital options for those who find that their lives fall short of their highest hopes. Literature is … our best goad toward new beginnings, our best chance of what we might call secular rebirth.'[15] This is a heavy load for literature to carry but it is a load that has fallen on its shoulders by default, and Edmundson's assessment of the role of literature is one way of saying, in secular terms, that the beauty of literature reflects the beauty of God and that literature's beauty can bring us to the paradise for which humans yearn. His book contains a short section on form. He points out that there are many ways to think of form. These include the Aristotelian view that the form of an object of art both sets up and satisfies a reader's expectations, as well as the Kantian view that form lifts the art object out of the regular push and pull of everyday life and makes it something that can be contemplated, studied and meditated upon in a disinterested manner. He then offers his own view about what form achieves for a work of literature, which is that form is the primary way in which writers infuse their words with feeling.[16] Form is the music of the work. This means, he says, that form is the sequence of notes that a sentence plays out; it is that which gives an emotional content to what would otherwise be a merely cognitive experience. This emotional content is the added spiritual tone of the work and the spiritual benefit resulting from reading it. On the bigger scale of the work, form is the grander, symphonic structure of the text that enable us to know what

---

15. Edmundson, *Why Read?*, pp. 2-3 (Edmundson's italics).
16. Ibid., p. 108.

it would be like to live out the work's vision. The example he gives is that of a Dickens novel. What he calls the astounding comic buoyancy of a Dickens novel, as well as the unflagging episodic inventiveness, sprawling variety and high-hearted tone, all contribute to the reader's capacity to sense what it would be like to live in Dickens's liberal world. Edmundson thus argues that the form of a novel creates and reveals emotion. Note, however, that form is understood here in both a micro and macro sense. The form of each sentence contributes to the overall form of a novel, and we can gain spiritual benefit from noticing both the big pattern of the book and the detailed pattern of sentence structure within it.

Form works in literature, according to Edmundson, because it summons up from within us feelings of one sort or another. Form plays on our emotions. He suggests that many readers will identify with protagonists who enter the world of the novel with strong desires but who find that experience knocks and even reverses those desires such that, in the end, they have been changed by the struggle of life and may emerge richer and better as a result. He also suggests that one of the reasons why Balzac's novels read as satisfyingly as they do is because his depiction of life as struggle, rivalry, triumph and bitter failure is in tune with traditional novelistic plotting. In contrast, he suggests that Don DeLillo also appeals to readers' emotions, in his case by departing from most of these traditional assumptions, such as choosing to shape his books without beginning, middle and end. DeLillo's destabilising technique challenges the readers to say what form or antiform might put them into the best place to make sense for themselves of their own life experience. Edmundson suggests that, whether reading traditionalist novels such as those by Balzac or transgressive ones such as DeLillo's, readers are, nevertheless, being set the same question: 'What is gained and what is lost when you map your life according to the archetypal plot – or when, in DeLillo's fashion, you refuse that mapping?'[17]

In short, the answer to this question might be that we can gain meaning and understanding, but there is also a risk that we might at the same time lose a proper sense of proportion. Edmundson expects that attempting to shape one's life according to the shape or shapelessness of novelistic plotting will lead only to frustration. The depiction of character, cause and effect in a novel might lead to readers

---

17. Ibid., p. 110.

idealising themselves and feeling inadequate because they do not live up to the literary model. On the other hand, such mirroring and shaping may be beneficial when they offer intensity and focus which help the reader to make meaning and find purpose. Edmundson calls this 'interfusion of feeling and thought' and he sees it as the essence of literary beauty. Aesthetic delight in this interfusion is the point of connectedness when the reader feels the author's truth and we know ourselves. Thus, interfusion is the key to the relationship between the form and the purpose of a text. It is the *distinctive* characteristic of literary beauty.

If we apply all the above to a recently published novel which raised critical interest in spring 2023, we shall see the way in which form, structure and style create literary beauty that appeals to the reader and draws us in, and the way in which gazing on literary beauty gives us glimpses of the numinous. The novel I have chosen for this is one whose subject is avowedly and unashamedly religious. This is *Cuddy*, Benjamin Myers's tenth novel, in which he experiments dexterously with the novel artform while exploring the influence St Cuthbert has exercised on Britain as a Christian nation over the centuries (although it could be argued that his influence has been greater over England than the other nations in Britain). By exploring Cuthbert's life and afterlife, he describes who we are as a nation, where we came from, how we have been shaped into what we are and, a reviewer suggested, perhaps also, the direction our nation might take in future.[18]

The Cuddy of the title is, of course, St Cuthbert, whose afterlife progress from his death on the Isle of Farne in 687 to his final resting places, one for his bones in Durham Cathedral, the other for his spiritual legacy in the hearts and minds of the English people, is the novel's main concern. The novel begins with his followers searching for a safe resting place for the saint's bones and the building of a cathedral to house them. A brief introduction traces the history of Cuthbert from his birth in Dunbar *circa* 634, his vision at the age of seventeen while he worked as a shepherd in Melrose monastery where he later became prior. In 665 he was appointed prior of Lindisfarne, a role from which he retired in 676 in search of a quieter life of religious devotion. Shortly before his death in 687 Cuthbert was persuaded out of retirement to

---

18. Nina Allan, 'Cuddy by Benjamin Myers Review: A Visionary History', *The Guardian*, 9 March 2023.

serve as bishop of Lindisfarne. When, a decade after his death, his body was found to be intact, he was declared a saint. Viking invasions a century later compelled his devotees to salvage his exhumed coffin and take it on a centuries-long peregrination throughout the north east of England until a permanent home could be found. Eventually, his followers settled on Durham and built the first of a series of churches. Durham still houses his much-venerated shrine.

To explore the role of beauty in the spirituality of reading I have chosen to focus on Myers's book, not only because it is expressly religious in subject and theme, but also because its author shows remarkable care for the art of fiction, as he plays with the novel form and employs quite a compendium of styles. The narrative of Cuthbert's life and long afterlife is told through four episodes: in book one the dead saint speaks to Ediva, who works as cook for his followers as, in 995, they carry his wooden coffin away from more Viking raids until she helps them identify a suitable, but perhaps temporary, resting place on a hill which she feels resembles Lindisfarne; book two tells of masons repairing Durham Cathedral's stonework in 1346; in book three, a sceptical professor finds his confidence in science challenged when the saint's tomb is opened for examination in 1827; and, in the final part, set in present times, a young poorly educated man, dependent for a meagre livelihood upon zero-hour work contracts, who lives with his dying mother in a village outside Durham, is offered a new job opportunity which brings him unexpected fresh insights into the world of the spiritual when he gets a lifting and carrying job at the cathedral.

These four books are augmented by a prologue and an interval. The prologue is voiced by Cuthbert himself at the moment of his death on 20 March 687. It is 'strange the way the dead mind works'.[19] Death comes only once, but at this moment 'a part of our lives / is death and the other dies in life'. His followers can be heard grieving: 'O Lord he is dead and now we are dead with him', but for Cuthbert his death is a homecoming, 'a surprise party'[20] he knew all along would, at some unknown time, be thrown in his honour. This prologue is a poetic imagining of the moment of dying, and in Cuthbert's final breath the dying man addresses us directly:

---

19. Benjamin Myers, *Cuddy* (London: Bloomsbury, 2023), p. 3.
20. Ibid., p. 6.

> But you
> *You*
> can call me
> Cuddy.[21]

Book one is told in the voice of Ediva, an orphan who had been taken in by the monks as a child and who travelled with them, not only as their cook, but also as a healer and helper. She is a visionary alive to the rhythm of the northern landscape in a way that distinguishes her from other young women. There is something mystical about her. Her driving vision is of a future cathedral 'bigger than anything man has ever built, so big it rears up like a mountain, like a great beast'.[22] Her words come to the reader in a free-flowing, unselfconscious stream straddling the border between poetry and prose, at times poetical in the style of Anglo-Saxon verse, at other times prosaic. Her final vision comes in the form of a short stanza:

> That night I have my final vision.
> I dream of a hill so great it is an
> island in the ocean of woodlands.
> On it is a cathedral made from a
> mountain. The cathedral I have
> seen all along. A place for Cuddy.[23]

After holding a vigil on the site, Ediva points out the place she has envisaged – 'a wooded island with the river snaked around its base' – and she pushes her sword deep into the heart of the hill as a 'marker for men'.[24]

In book two Fletcher Bullard, a champion archer, is away fighting the Scots when his wife Eda meets Francis Rolfe, one of a team of masons engaged in 1346 in the task of repairing the decorative stonework around the cathedral. Bullard, 'a man-beast so large in life to be a living myth in the minds of all those who meet him',[25] is an abuser at home and a bully outdoors. With an epigraph taken from

---

21. Ibid., p. 7.
22. Ibid., p. 55.
23. Ibid., p. 163.
24. Ibid., p. 166.
25. Ibid., p. 262.

the northern writer, Basil Bunting's *Briggflatts* (1966), in which it is claimed that, because pens are too light, one must take a chisel to write, this section of the novel is set out with slabs of text of various lengths without paragraph indentations on each page, like blocks of stone carved out in the book. The solidity of the text on the page matches the brutality of the medieval story it tells, at the climax of which Bullard flees to the cathedral to grasp the sanctuary knocker that promised safety from harm for anyone who claimed it. What has happened is that, on his return from Scotland, Bullard has found Eda pregnant by Rolfe and exercised his jealous vengeance against both his wife and her lover. He is a wanted man. At the end of the section, rumours abound that Bullard was granted sanctuary and that he had set sail from Hartlepool to freedom overseas, but there are also contrary rumours that the monks had taken him into the fields around Durham to do 'unspeakable and imaginative things'[26] to him. If true, the monks will themselves need to answer to God for this breach of the law of sanctuary. Marks in the stone, which had been repaired by Rolfe, high out of sight, perpetuate the story of Eda and his love for her, as does the name chosen for their son – Cuthbert.

The Interlude takes the form of a drama script in which the cathedral itself gives a voiceover recording of what was done to it when three thousand Scottish soldiers were imprisoned within its walls in September 1650 after their defeat by Cromwell's Parliamentarians in the battle of Dunbar. Most of the incarcerated men were 'honey-fed farm boys and moor-top dreamers', who experienced ill-treatment at the hands of their Parliamentarian conquerors. In 2013, the construction of a cathedral café revealed a mass grave proving that as many as 1,700 prisoners perished as a result of starvation, illness or injury. 'The cathedral had lost its purpose as a place of worship, sanctity and sanctuary for all comers.'[27] This Interlude depicts the low point in the cathedral's history, an ignoble and sacrilegious chapter in its story. Unlike this section of unremitting darkness, all other sections of the novel tell of the survival of goodness and grace even during times of violence and corruption. Some light always shines through. I guess that this explains why Myers designated it as an Interlude rather than a fifth book. It does not contain the connecting

---

26. Ibid., p. 264.
27. Ibid., p. 269.

tropes of the main chapters; it is distinctive. It is indeed an interlude allowing the cathedral itself to speak.

Book three is a pastiche of the Victorian ghost story, said by Nina Allan in her review of the novel, to be all the more satisfying because it is populated by ghosts we have already met.[28] It includes passages imitating epistolary novels of the period. In this section, an Oxford professor, Forbes Fawcett-Black, is invited to witness the opening of Cuthbert's tomb in 1827. He travels north reluctantly, because he regards the region as 'a distant universe, a faraway celestial plane onto which little light penetrated',[29] and he is suspicious of every stranger he meets there. However, his time in the north changes him forever. Previously sceptical of anything except science, he ends up believing in God. When all his experiences in the north are over, he does not know what became of the remains of St Cuthbert but he is forever haunted by imagined hearings of the chanting of the saint's followers, he feels that God always looks on and he resigns his post as professor of antiquities.

The final part of the novel finds Myers writing in his more natural gritty and earthy style familiar to readers of his previous novels. The grim north is evoked in the strong stench of urine in the bus stations where Michael Cuthbert waits for a lift to work, in the Pot Noodles he grabs from the kitchen cabinet as he leaves the house because there are no shops or facilities where he works, and in Myers's description of the driver spitting phlegm through the car window. Michael sneaks away at the lunch break to ring his mother, and we see the full import of this caring conversation when he returns after work and we discover that he is his dying mother's principal carer, now emptying the bedpan that had awaited his return and making sure she has eaten and has something to drink. The foreman at the dead-end, zero-hours demolition job offers him a labouring job at the cathedral and this turns out to be Michael's big unexpected break. His care for his mother is heart-rending, especially in her final moments when he converses with St Cuthbert who makes his final appearance in the novel he has inhabited throughout.

At other points in the novel, Cuddy's voice is heard in dreams, carried on the wind and the sound of the sea, and passed down the generations through the memories and cherished relics of those who

---

28. Allan, 'Cuddy by Benjamin Myers Review'.
29. Myers, *Cuddy*, p. 284.

preceded the characters in each section. Yet there are many more connections between the chapters than Cuthbert's voice: Ediva, the tenth-century cook, becomes Eda, the stonemason's wife in 1364, Edith, a cathedral housekeeper in 1827, and Evie, a student waitress in the café, in 2019. Her original companion, Owl Eyes, appears in later sections as a husband and as Daft Lad in the final section. Moreover, in each section there is a bad monk and a violent man.

In *Cuddy*, form and beauty are present at both macro and micro levels – in the overall structure of the book, with recurring images, themes and characters, and in the detailed linguistic stylistics of each section. The overall form of the novel achieves for the reader a sense of the lasting and deep influence of this northern saint on the region he adopted when he moved there as a young man and where he died. As Nina Allan said, 'The symbiosis of poetry and story, of knowledge and deep love, marks out *Cuddy* as a singular and significant achievement',[30] which offers a 'state of the nation' commentary, showing not only whence we came, but perhaps also beginning to map out the nation's future.

Nevertheless, a destabilising observation must yet be made. Published and received as a novel, *Cuddy*'s various sections are interleaved with bibliographical references ranging from the Venerable Bede to Simon Schama, from Alcuin to Magnus Magnusson. Novels – all novels – are underpinned with research, some done more conscientiously than others, but sections in *Cuddy* that leave Myers's extensive research exposed, like the visible architectural underpinnings in an accessible cathedral crypt, risk historicising the book and compromising its fictiveness. Myers dodges this risk because he gives readers much to admire. We admire the artistry of the author's telling as much as we admire the devotion and sanctity of the saint whose longer-than-life story he tells. We admire the form of the book and the detailed stylistics of each section. We admire its beauty on the grand scale and in its detail. The literary beauty of this religious story spanning more than a millennium draws us close to the beauty of holiness, the beauty of God. It brings us to the brink of worship. It almost tips us over from the act of reading into prayer.

A hymn by Cyril Allington (1872-1955), 'Lord of beauty, Thine the splendour', sees God's beauty reflected in 'earth and sky and sea'. This is a conventional thought often expressed in liturgy and hymnody, but

---

30. Allan, 'Cuddy by Benjamin Myers Review'.

the prayer of Allington's last verse, that our purified vision will render God glorified in *all things*, extends the thought beyond natural beauty alone, to embrace literary beauty, a point not missed when we note that Allington's interest, as a scholarly clergyman, lay in literature as much as it did in theology. Allington encapsulates the argument of this chapter: God's beauty is evident in literary aesthetics, and such beauty feeds the soul.

9

Contemplative Reading

A report that *The New York Times* begins every morning's news meeting with a poetry reading to inspire its journalists and boost their creativity sparked some interesting comments. One of its picture editors remarked that the poetry often jolted his mind into thinking about a subject in an unexpected way; the poet Don Peterson commented that a good poem can draw you out of a rut and remind you how to get people to pay attention to what you want to say; and another said that the poetry reading opened to those who listened other ways of using language and getting beyond clichés and soundbites. Most interesting for us is Roger McGough's comparison with school assemblies, in what he called the olden days, in which the school day began with prayers. For McGough, both the school assembly and the newsroom poetry reading are moments of thoughtfulness which take your mind elsewhere and help you see whatever you will encounter that day with refocussed eyes.[1] One art form – poetry – sheds light on another, more ephemeral, art form – journalism.

The technical term for art reflecting on art is ekphrasis. *The New York Times* experiment is not purely ekphrasis, but it is not far removed from it. Ekphrasis is, most usually, a literary reflection on a visual work of art, a prose section or poem describing or meditating on a painting or sculpture. It is an ancient practice – Homer's description of the shield of Achilles in *The Iliad* is an early example – but it seems

---

1. Frances Perraudin, 'Bard Labour: Boost Workplace Productivity "by Reading a Poem"', *The Guardian*, 6 March 2020.

to me to have become much more common in recent decades as a greater variety of modern arts, such as film, have been developed. The term comes from the Greek for 'speak out' and refers to naming an inanimate object. The idea is that the secondary artist is calling out what the primary artist merely implied in the original work. The secondary work amplifies the first.

An obvious well-known example is John Keats's *Ode on a Grecian Urn*, where the poet observes in minute detail the 'leaf-fring'd legend' that adorns the vase, asking who are the men, maidens and deities that struggle to escape their clay forms. Keats reflects that their silent music and static shapes are far above 'all breathing human passion', their youthfulness cannot fade and their love will be eternal. The 'marble men and maidens overwrought' portrayed on the urn speak to the poet and teach him that, 'Beauty is truth, truth beauty, – that is all / Ye know on earth, and all ye need to know.' Who could ever know whether the creator of the ancient vase was wedded to this philosophy? Probably not. It is Keats's philosophy; and it is Romantic. However, the literary or rhetorical practice of ekphrasis has drawn from one work of art, the vase, another work of art: one of the most famous poems in the English literary canon. The first is the subject, the second is the actor of the ekphrasis.

Ekphrasis can involve almost any artistic medium as its subject and almost any other artistic medium as its actor. A painting can reflect on a sculpture, a film on a novel, a piece of music on a collection of paintings, a symphony on a narrative, a photograph on a ceramic and so on. The possibilities are almost endless but the most common, I would say, is the use of poetry acting on almost any other art form to draw out some aspect of its meaning or significance. This chapter explores the practice of ekphrasis as a tool for spiritual enjoyment, a means to deepen spirituality.

I should express an important caveat which is that Paul Cézanne said that talking about art is virtually useless.[2] I take this to mean that any art form should be allowed to speak for itself in its own terms and that when music, for instance, is being discussed verbally that takes something away from the music even if the intention is to explicate the music in some way. Words cannot replace music or pictures, even if some would say that the pictures are better on the radio.

---

2. Used as the epigram to Maitreyabandhu's anthology of poetry, *After Cézanne* (Hexham: Bloodaxe Books, 2019).

The value of ekphrasis, however, is that it creates a secondary art form that develops and gives a new life form to the original. If Keats's poem had been inspired by looking at a specific Greek vase, the vase could still be admired in its own terms. His poem has not denigrated it in any way. Nor has the poem necessarily become a substitute for the vase. Rather, the ode has become a new work of art, related to the original and helps anyone who appreciates the poem also to appreciate the vase. Ekphrasis thus has significant potential for a spirituality of reading. Certain spiritual practices relating to ekphrasis can be developed, and to get there this chapter will explore the work of four recent and contemporary practitioners of ekphrasis. These are the poets, Maitreyabandhu, R.S. Thomas and W.H. Auden, and a short prose writer and editor, Lawrence Block.[3]

I want to begin with Maitreyabandhu because, as a Buddhist teacher, his work is free of any specifically Christian undertones. It, therefore, leads us into the value of ekphrasis for spirituality in a more general manner, before I zone in on Christian spirituality.

* * *

Maitreyabandhu studied fine art at Goldsmith's College in London and now teaches Buddhism and meditation in the London Buddhist Centre, so his sequence of 56 poems reflecting on Cézanne's post-impressionist paintings seems a natural step for this poet.[4] The poetry explores the paintings in relation to Cézanne's life and afterlife. In it Maitreyabandhu reimagines the artist's friendships with Zola and Pissarro, his professional influence on Matisse and Picasso, and his posthumous reputation. In choosing to focus on this artist's work, Maitreyabandhu takes up a task an earlier poet might have taken on: Rainer Maria Rilke, for example, especially admired the artist's watercolours when he saw them in Paris and could readily have chosen to do what Maitreyabandhu has now done. Cézanne's specific themes were bathers, card players, landscapes and still life paintings and, from these, Maitreyabandhu uses the rhetorical device of ekphrasis to draw out hidden narratives, points of relation to Cézanne's own life and lessons for our lives. As Barnaby Wright says on the back cover of

---

3. I also considered Ciaran Carson's *Still Life* (Salem, MA: Wake Forest University Press, 2020).
4. Maitreyabandhu's *After Cézanne*, reviewed by John Greening in the *Times Literary Supplement*, 21 March 2020, p. 32.

the anthology, the poems show the close kinship between poetry and painting. The insights into Cézanne's work within the poetry might have only been grasped through poetry. The sequence of poems is dependent in every respect upon the visual art, not always depicted on the same page but sometimes elsewhere in this illustrated book.

'Man with a Pipe' is placed opposite a depiction of Cézanne's *Man with a Pipe* (1892-95), '[A]s if the human heart had these two sides', the visual and the verbal. The opening line of the poem refers to the portrait sitter's waistcoat and sets the pattern for Maitreyabandhu's close observation of the picture. He notes that the face is in shadow but one ear is in a better light, that the workman's shoulders are set wide apart, that the shirt collar is tucked in although one side is not depicted, that the shirt is 'grimed with tobacco-sweat', that the man's jacket is the colour of 'topsoil and clay', not 'merely brown or grey', and that the pipe is 'clenched and brittle'.[5] Furthermore, he imagines that his coat's 'cuffs are thin and frayed (if we could see them)'. He cannot possibly know this for the portrait is cut off just above elbow level.

I begin with this poem because it demonstrates Maitreyabandhu's ability to imagine a narrative from a portrait of an unidentified man, a narrative of humanity God-breathed into life from the dust of the earth to become 'the common man / old reprobate and lover'. The poem does indeed refer to the Genesis story, a rare occurrence among these poems. This explains the two sides of the man's heart referred to in the poem's opening line in which the poet says one side advances while the other retreats, this being a feature of the human condition: we are both from somewhere and on our way to somewhere else. Like the man's pipe, which Maitreyabandhu suggests has been 'dropped into a bean drill' many a time, we, too, can be lost and found again.

Religious or spiritual insights particular to specific religions only rarely show through any of the poems in *After Cézanne*. Maitreyabandhu even keeps his Buddhism in the background, except occasionally, such as in 'Einstein's Watch'. This poem draws on a comment made by Albert Einstein and Leopold Infeld in their popular book tracing the development of ideas in physics, *The Evolution of Physics* (1938). They compared the human endeavour to understand reality to someone trying to understand the mechanism of a closed watch without opening it. The poem also draws on Rilke's experience

---

5. Maitreyabandhu, *After Cézanne*, p. 43.

when he first encountered Cézanne's work. The paintings puzzled him and he felt insecure but there came a time when 'suddenly one has the right eyes'.[6] Much longer than 'Man with a Pipe', 'Einstein's Watch' combines allusions to 'Milton's God looking down with mercy / and regret' with a typically Buddhist critique of contemporary worldly existence in which the poet reckons the 'everyday pornography of fact … condemns our agency and bric-à-brac of thought / to meagre usefulness, to usefulness and want'.[7] All that can be seen, touched and tasted is a mere 'happenstance of sense' and the pond life the poet can see in Cézanne's painting 'speak[s] / volumes for our tomfoolery and lust'. The artist sees better than we do because he looks harder and longer than we do. We should be more willing to look closely, to open the watch to examine it rather than 'guess / at causes, picture cogs and inner workings / so it fits with everything we know' but 'because we can't remove the back' we live with assumptions, true or false, and for want to careful contemplation, we 'will never / know for sure the world we say we're sure of'. What it all comes back to in the end, says the poet in this first-person colloquy, 'is that "suddenly one has the right eyes …"' The practice of Buddhist meditation, in common with all spiritual practices, is to learn to acquire eyes that can see beyond meagre utilitarianism to reality beyond.

Cézanne's portrait of his wife, *Madame Cézanne in Blue* (1888-90), a portrait of similar scale and perspective as *Man with a Pipe*, inspires a poem in which Maitreyabandhu imagines Rainer Maria Rilke writing to his wife about a conversation he had with Count Kessler, a diplomat and art patron, as they stood before some paintings in a Parisian gallery. It is entitled 'Rilke Writes to His Wife from the Salon d'Automne'.[8] At several points in the poem he quotes from an actual letter of Rilke's. Like *Man with a Pipe*, the painting is reproduced opposite the poem in this collection, and the poem also relies on close observation.

The poet observes that this picture is truncated above the sitter's wrists and the background is in two halves, one light and the other dark. He uses Kessler's critique of the portrait in an imagined conversation with Rilke to draw our attention to the 'petal-like white collar' of Mme Cézanne's blouse which accentuates her beauty. Her

---

6. Ibid., p. 106.
7. Ibid., p. 54.
8. Ibid., p. 67.

head is tilted and her eyes mismatched, and yet he must have loved her much, says Kessler, to make her look so rich 'in her bourgeois cotton blue' (a quotation from Rilke's actual letter) 'and counterpointed face'. He sees the mordancy and sadness in her face before he tugs at Rilke's arm and asks him, 'And have you noticed this? ... The wallpaper, its clumsy pattern fills the right-hand corner / Now what does it remind you of ... [sic] tears?' He draws our attention to a partially obscured shelf bracket which 'breaks the picture's logic' and almost appears to hold her head in its stillness. This, he suggests, captures 'our hankering and fear, / our common lot'. Now Rilke writes to his wife and expresses the thought that Mme Cézanne is 'imprisoned in an afterlife / of paint', not at all sure why she, or anyone else, is given to suffer. The poem, and Rilke's imagined letter to his wife, concludes with three quotations from an actual letter from Rilke: 'one lives so badly coming into the present unfinished', 'It's still raining extravagantly outside' and 'Only this ... for Sunday.'

Mme Cézanne's stillness and silence, frozen in a moment of sadness, fixed in a present time which is no more speaks to me, but only through Maitreyabandhu's poem, of our incompleteness unless we bring our past into the present and take our present into a fluid future. The state of desertion in which Mme Cézanne was portrayed need not be forever. The poem also hinges on the word 'unsightly' which Maitreyabandhu adds to Rilke's observation about being unfinished: 'One lives so badly coming into the present unfinished, unsightly.' Is this 'unsightly' intended to mean 'unseen' or 'not pleasing to see'? Do we live badly when we do not look carefully enough and miss seeing something? Do we live badly when we do not look through the art to the unseen beyond? Or do we live badly when we do not look at whatever makes humanity suffer? Looking carefully, concentratedly, meditatively will free us from the prison of what the poet calls 'the darker side'. Holy attention, careful observation of the painting by the poet, has revealed the inner depths of the art.

Opposite a photograph of a still life, *The Blue Vase* (1889-90), Maitreyabandhu writes four stanzas entitled 'Human Things'.[9] The poet's notes state that the poem refers also to *Tulips in a Vase* (1892). The poem begins with close observation of the first of these still lifes, noticing that, if one lifted the window blind behind the vase, the room would fill with winter light and turn objects on the

---

9. Ibid., p. 57.

mantelpiece into treasures. Observing that the vase leans slightly to the left, he infers that what we thought was 'fixed and stable is in flux'. In contrast with this misshapen vase, Cézanne took more care and time over 'human things'.

The poem ends with a Homeric allusion: *Ut pictura poesis*, which translates as 'As is painting, so is poetry.' This seems to serve as the philosophy underpinning the *After Cézanne* sequence, and Homer nods in agreement: '*Ut pictura poesis*: mute poetry / (and even Homer nods).' The paradox with which this poem concludes both undermines and underpins Maitreyabandhu's enterprise. As in Homer, an early practitioner of ekphrasis, the poetry carries the same force of painting, and yet the poetry is mute. Perhaps the painting is also unseen until the poetry calls it out.

Another recurring theme in Cézanne's oeuvre is self-portraiture, and one of the last poems in Maitreyabandhu's sequence meditates on what is thought to be Cézanne's final *Self Portrait with a Beret* (1898-99), on which the poet writes 'Two Ways of Closing'.[10] This is also inspired by the painter describing himself as a painter 'still game' or 'still vigorous' in a letter of 1903.[11] Moreover, the poet imagines the artist, portrayed in right profile, gazing to the right of the painting at another of his paintings, *Three Skulls on an Oriental Rug* (1898), which he may have been working on at the same time. It could still have been in his studio. A portrait of a living person is thus placed alongside a depiction of death, leading the poet to write of 'fruits that ripen, fall, and flower again' in the cycle of life and death. The two paintings 'balance life and death on a shifting stage / like a cosmogram for deliberate regard'. So, says Maitreyabandhu, Cézanne 'finds his answer one last time: / hands down and beretted, he seems to say / we have come this far, lately, lately and hard'.

To pick up the imagery of 'Two Ways of Closing', the poems and paintings in *After Cézanne* are laid out before us like a cosmogram. These are two-dimensional geometric figures depicting a cosmology of some sort, perhaps representing the earth or the universe. They can be diagrammatic or pictorial, and many cultures and religions use them. Labyrinths outside cathedrals in medieval Christendom and the pictorial map featured in many editions of John Bunyan's *Pilgrim's Progress* are among Christian examples, while the complex

---

10. Ibid., p. 99.
11. Ibid., p. 110.

design of mandalas are used in many religious traditions as foci for meditation and contemplation. In a similar manner, the poetry and the visual art of *After Cézanne* are laid before us to gaze upon.

Having seen how ekphrasis works in the poetry of a Buddhist teacher, we now turn to a Christian poet whose reputation is that of a dour depicter of Welsh peasantry and apophatic theology but, nonetheless, whose appreciation of the visual arts found expression in two collections of poetry. He is R.S. Thomas, and the ekphrastic anthologies are *Between Here and Now* (1981) and *Ingrowing Thoughts* (1985).

In 1963 Thomas edited *The Penguin Book of Religious Verse*. In his introduction he wrote:

> It is not necessarily the poems couched in conventionally religious language that convey the truest religious experience. ... Are we not coming to accept that, wherever and whenever man broods upon himself and his destiny, he does it as a spiritual and self-conscious being without peer in the universe which we know?

Many of Thomas's ekphrastic poems seem superficially less spiritual than some of his other poems yet nowhere else does his specific spiritual interest show itself more strongly in such a way that we see through to the invisible world. Standing in front of works of art a viewer's imagination is most revealingly exercised. Or, as D.Z. Phillips implied, talk of God can only be possible if we do not ignore life's central features.[12] Talk of God can only inform human life if we have looked at both the beauty and the horror of it, often as it is expressed in art.

Phillips also suggested that the key to the poems in *Between Here and Now* is the final poem in the collection, 'Threshold', and this not only because its title is a precise description of where the poet and the reader stand in relation to the art but also because the human condition itself is a threshold existence.[13] The collection is in two parts, the first 33 poems form a self-contained set called 'Impressions', each one responding to one of the 33 Impressionist and Post-Impressionist

---

12. D.Z. Phillips, *R.S. Thomas: Poet of the Hidden God: Meaning and Mediation in the Poetry of RS Thomas* (London: Macmillan, 1986), p. 138.
13. Ibid., p. 152.

paintings reproduced in monochrome on the verso page. On the whole, unlike Maitreyabandhu's *After Cézanne*, Thomas's poems would be quite unintelligible without seeing the paintings, upon which they are more closely dependent. In many instances, some aspects of the art, especially technique, go unmentioned in the poetry. A second section called 'Other Poems', raising expectation of an unrelated miscellany, is not as random a collection as one might expect. Instead, they are related to the main issues raised in the first section, so the final poem, 'Threshold', can indeed be read as intentionally conclusive.

'Threshold'[14] begins with an allusion to the biblical narrative in which Elijah, after spending a night in a cave, is beckoned to stand on Mount Horeb as 'the Lord is about to pass by' (1 Kings 19:11). A mighty hurricane blows, the earth quakes, and a mighty inferno rages, but Elijah does not detect God in any of these. Standing at the mouth of the cave, Elijah hears God in 'a sound of sheer silence' (1 Kings 19:12). The poet similarly emerges from 'the mind's cave' and, outside, 'where things pass', he fails to encounter God: 'the Lord is in none of them'. The still, small voice he hears is 'that of the bacteria destroying [his] cosmos'. The threshold on which he lingers, analogous to the mouth of the cave in the Elijah narrative, is the only place he can stand, for where else can he go? 'To look back is to lose the soul / I was leading upward towards / the light.' His question, 'To look forward?', remains enigmatically unanswered. His precarious human predicament is to balance at the edge of an abyss between what has passed and what is to come. What else can he do but reach out, like Adam in Michelangelo's Sistine Chapel ceiling, into 'unknown space, hoping for the reciprocating touch'? Indeed, in each poem in 'Impressions' the poet has reached out to the paintings and sought reciprocation between the arts; he stands in the gap between, on the threshold. In this respect his ekphrastic poetry is more in keeping with the rest of his oeuvre than we might have first thought. These poems confirm Thomas as a looking, staring poet: all his poetry is an effort to reach a better understanding of the human condition, as well as a striving to move deeper into God, while he wrestled with both the finiteness of humanity and the inadequacies of our language. What we find in his poetry is that life is transfigured by art and art transfigures spirituality. Let us observe the transfiguration ekphrasis is capable

---

14. R.S. Thomas, *Between Here and Now* (London: Macmillan, 1981), p. 110.

of achieving as we consider five examples of Thomas's impressions of the Impressionists.

First, 'Pissarro: Landscape at Chaponval',[15] a rural scene portraying a woman tending a cow at the base of a hill, is divided into four horizontal bands: the field where the cow grazes at the base; houses at the bottom of the hill; the hillside above; and, at top, a sky with clouds. The woman and the cow, entirely within the lowest band of grass, are framed to the left by a tree which is the full height of the picture and a sapling to the right. The poem's opening line, 'It would be good to live ...', reminds me of the synoptic Gospel accounts of Christ's transfiguration where after the vision, in each account, Peter, wanting to prolong the experience by building a permanent shelter, says, 'It is good for us to be here.' Although the conditional tense 'would' in the first line of the poem shows that the poet knows there can be no lasting dwelling place in the art, transfiguration is one of the themes of this poem. Thomas reads the picture from top to bottom. Beginning with the village, the hill and the clouds above, he ends with the grass, the woman and the cow, describing the grass as 'a tide / rising and falling' with the seasons. He says the cow sips the grass, slowly filling her udders.

This scene evokes two images, one from within Thomas's own work, the other a well-known poetic image for the tide of religious faith. In Thomas's poem 'The Other', originally published untitled, he writes of lying awake in the night 'listening / to the swell born somewhere in the Atlantic / rising and falling, rising and falling' leading him to think of 'that other being who is awake, too, / letting our prayers break in on him'.[16] The significance of this poem is evidenced in that it was chosen to be inscribed on a slate in the churchyard of Aberdaron where Thomas was priest for eleven years, as well as alongside his obituary in the *Guardian* newspaper. The other image evoked comes from Matthew Arnold, who, in the middle years of the nineteenth century, wrote of 'The Sea of Faith ... Its melancholy, long, withdrawing roar' retreating to the edges of the earth ('Dover Beach', 1867). Despite the repeated rising and falling, what predominates in the Pissarro poem is the expressed initial desire to live in that village where 'time [is] stationary'. This sense of the stillness of

---

15. Ibid., pp. 44-45.
16. R.S. Thomas, *Collected Poems: 1945-1990* (London: J.M. Dent, 1993), p. 457.

Contemplative Reading

time is accentuated if we consider that the cowherd is like the poet waiting by the cistern of observation, meditation and distillation for the harmony and fulfilment when the human, animal, natural and spiritual worlds come together in a moment of transfiguration. Such is the transfiguring effect of art on our lives.

Van Gogh's 'The Church at Auvers'[17] is the subject of the second poem we consider. The painting is dominated by the bulk of a church which the poem regards as being 'so large ... / for so small / a village'. On a path running around the church a woman walks by. The poet notes that the church 'divides the path / as a rock / in mid-stream' and that the woman is not going to the church. Alluding to his Welsh poet-priest predecessor, George Herbert, whose 'Elixir' saw vocation in the labours of a servant 'Who sweeps a room as for Thy laws', Thomas sees that the woman's work, also sweeping rooms and scrubbing floors, must be done somewhere other than the church. The overall effect of both the poem and the painting is to identify a gulf between church and world. It is as if the church is an obstacle to the path around it and the church with its 'uncaring belfry' shows only indifference to the woman bustling by.

We encounter this division yet again when Thomas responds to 'Gauguin: The Alyscamps at Arles'.[18] In this instance the division is between the stiff formality of churchy religions and the free expression of nature and art. In the centre of Gauguin's picture are three figures who have the stiffness of candles. Thomas calls them 'a trinity of figures – / coming from Mass?' They had attended church out of convention, but now, both in the freedom found outside church and within Gauguin's free expression of art, Thomas recognises the sense of liberation and consequent celebration which is found lacking inside the church. It is the freedom of a different form of sacrament from the Mass, the sacrament of art. 'Art is a sacrament / in itself', he says. Between them, the poet and the artist manifest a visible expression of invisible truths, lift the veil on a hidden God, and begin a eucharistic 'celebration of colour'.

This is so because, as we see when we turn to a fourth poem in the collection, 'Degas: Women Ironing', art is eternal.[19] The painting portrays two laundry workers, one grossly yawning while holding

---
17. Thomas, *Between Here and Now*, pp. 64-65.
18. Ibid., pp. 58-59.
19. Ibid., pp. 52-53.

a bottle of wine, the other sunk in tiredness and hunched over her ironing. It is a rather unappealing portrait of ordinary life. As the poem is a response to the art, so the painting is Degas's response to what he sees. The poem is set out on the page with alternate lines indented, so the reader's eyes, going back and forth from one line to the next, mimic the action of ironing, a soporific motion in one laundress, dulled by wine, in the other exhausted by labour. In contrast, both Degas and Thomas are alert and observant. Degas gives them no less attention than he would an aristocratic sitter. The active laundress lacks spiritual dignity, for her hands are not clasped in prayer but pressing down on a hot iron, and her work is demeaning, employed as she is in a 'decreasing / function'. Yet this painting is art. Indeed, this art permanently overcomes any temptation we might have 'to answer / a yawn with a yawn'. These women merit the artist's attention; they deserve to be immortalised by him. Degas's painting rewards the poet's attention; and the poem rewards ours, for we see beauty in the mundane, dignity in working women and eternity in a moment of time.

Finally, 'Van Gogh: Portrait of Dr Gachet'[20] is a melancholic portrait inspiring Thomas to locate his poem both in his own time and in the time of Dr Gachet. He regards the physician both as a doctor and the subject of an art work. The doctor is alone, '[n]ot part of the Health Service', and, without colleagues, unable to consult anyone. Picking up on the way the doctor rests his cheek on his arm and elbow as if listening to someone on the telephone or listening through a stethoscope to detect the symptoms of a disease, the poet notices how the doctor listens to life. He listens to life as it describes its symptoms. His left hand rests on a foxglove, source of the medicine, digitalis, but described by Thomas as 'equivocal' because foxgloves are both therapeutic and toxic. Like Dr Gachet we apprehend life through our senses, and it is the role of art – in all its many forms – to help us to diagnose life's ills and remedy society's problems. This recognition that we live life through our senses is what promotes almost any artistic enterprise.

Four years later Thomas took up a similar task in *Ingrowing Thoughts*, this time offering 20 poems that meditate on twentieth-century Surrealist, Cubist and Post-Expressionist paintings. In this

---

20. Ibid., pp. 62-63.

collection he alternated the location of the paintings between the verso and recto pages so that sometimes the poem illogically comes before the painting.

Although standing out within Thomas's oeuvre as a distinct genre, none of his ekphrastic poems breaks with his spiritual tradition, his theological outlook or his religious interests. They continue the impression of him as a poet of waiting, living on the margins, at the threshold of life, never more than glimpsing the divine and unable to put in words the ineffable. In these poems, he remains the poet of the hidden God, *deus absconditus*, keeping watch for the twitch of the curtains that betrays a presence within, sniffing the air for the scent of the divine who has just left the room, and listening out for a faint echo of prayer answered. He is also doing this when contemplating and responding to pictures. His apophatic theology remains uncompromised in any way by concrete art.

Possibly the best-known poem meditating on a work of art – and perhaps the most referenced in church circles because of what it reveals about the human experience of suffering and the theological dilemma it creates – is W.H. Auden's 'Musée des Beaux Arts' (1938). Arthur Kirsch describes it as 'one of the greatest poems ever written on painting'[21] and it would feel negligent not to spend some time with it now. In a sermon Auden preached in Westminster Abbey in 1966, Auden argued for close observance of the created world and human society. This, he said, is because, by that stage, science had demythologised the universe. He compared our observation of natural phenomena to his own task when reading a poem, where he encounters the author's words not the author. Similarly, he said, we encounter the created world not the creator. At the beginning of his sermon, therefore, Auden spelled out that this did not mean that he held 'a Gnostic religiosity which would have us avert our eyes from the created phenomenal word to gaze at its Creator whom no man hath seen at any time – which is as if a man were to say – O I never listen to Mozart symphonies because it distracts me from thinking about Mozart'.[22] Auden wants us to look at art, the natural world and

---

21. Arthur Kirsch, *Auden and Christianity* (New Haven, CT: Yale University Press, 2005), p. 19.
22. Quoted in ibid., pp. 162-63.

human experience although, as windows on their creators, they are but clouded glass.

In 'Musée des Beaux Arts' Auden visits the Brussels gallery of that name and, surveying Pieter Breughel the Elder's work, shows his desire to understand Christianity in the context of ordinary day-to-day human experience. What interests him here is 'the human position' on the matter of suffering – what we might more naturally call the human condition or predicament of nature and society's disinterest in a person's downfall and the way in which that person suffers as a result. In the first stanza, Auden moves around the exhibition to view at least four, possibly five, Breughel paintings.

In two, *The Census at Bethlehem* (1566) and *The Adoration of the Kings in the Snow* (1567), the arrival of Mary and Joseph in Bethlehem in the former, and the visitation of the Magi in the latter, are almost lost amidst the multitude of Netherlandish townsfolk that populate the busy scenes. They are going about their business while something eventful 'run[s] its course / Anyhow in a corner'. In both paintings, children who may not have looked out for the momentous birth of Christ, continue to play on the ice. In the allusion to children 'skating / On a pond at the edge of a wood', Auden may have also been thinking of *Winter Landscape with Skaters and a Bird Trap* (1565), which portrays children skating on a pond and a rather vicious trap for killing birds. The stanza also calls up Breughel's *The Massacre of the Innocents* (1566) in which 'dogs go on with their doggy life', while soldiers, some mounted on horses and others on foot, become torturers who snatch children from their mothers and slay them in the snow. Men, women and animals look on and do nothing to stop the massacre, although I have been unable to spot in any of the paintings the horse Auden mentions 'scratch[ing] its innocent behind on a tree'. Dogs also pursue their doggy lives in *The Procession to Calvary* (1564). In this painting Christ drags his cross almost unnoticed through the crowds of people who are heading for the place of execution tucked in the top right-hand corner of the painting. Most are minding their own business and some are walking out of the picture. Even John and the three Marys, in the foreground in the bottom right of the painting, have turned their backs on Christ, though they are consumed by grief rather than indifferent like the other figures. All the human figures in Breughel's art are ordinary folk, and the divine subjects mingle among them appearing no different from anyone else. They have no halos or any other marker of significance. Only the artist's looking, the poet's looking and our looking show any difference.[23] Such is the power of contemplative observation.

The second stanza of Auden's poem specifies *Landscape with the Fall of Icarus* (c. 1560) as its subject, and Auden examines it carefully, pulling into focus the theology of suffering he had observed in the other paintings. The artwork shows a shepherd leaning on his crook, accompanied by his dog and surrounded by sheep, a ploughman cutting a furrow, a fisherman tending his line and a ship sailing by, none of them distracted or moved by the remarkable sight of the fall from the sky of a flying man whose flailing white legs disappear into the sea. The power of this poem, says Kirsch, lies in 'the juxtaposition of momentous suffering with the unconcerned lives of ordinary people'.[24] Breughel depicts disinterested humanity but Auden's poem provokes a more compassionate response to the downfall of Icarus and, indeed, to any instance of human suffering by alerting us to our callousness. When we hear a 'forsaken cry', Auden implicitly begs us not to 'sail calmly on' without stopping to help. Another poet reflecting on the same work of art, William Carlos Williams, was more direct than Auden and shocked his readers into recognising that the 'splash quite unnoticed' was 'Icarus drowning' ('Landscape with the Fall of Icarus', 1962).

Now, lest I leave you with the impression that ekphrasis is mainly poetry reflecting on art, let me take you to the last room visitors enter when attending an art gallery: the gift shop. In one of these a couple of years ago, the friend I was with persuaded me to look at a collection of short stories edited by an American suspense and fiction writer, Lawrence Block, after we had toured an exhibition of Edward Hopper paintings.[25] Each story in the specially commissioned collection was inspired by one of the paintings, each of which is printed in glossy colour as the title page of the story related to it. Edward Hopper, who was born in upstate New York and died in New York City, flourished as an artist from the 1920s to the 1960s. Many of his paintings depict lone individuals observed in their interior solitariness, through windows,

---

23. See Gerard Loughlin, 'The Man Who Fell to Earth', in *The Blackwell Companion to Postmodern Theology*, ed. Graham Ward (Oxford: Blackwell, 2001), p. 34.
24. Kirsch, *Auden and Christianity*, p. 20.
25. Lawrence Block, ed., *In Sunlight or in Shadow: Stories Inspired by the Paintings of Edward Hopper* (New York, NY: Pegasus Books, 2016).

veranda railings or doorways. They are moody, intense portraits of people who seem to be either drawn in on themselves or awaiting the arrival of another. In his editorial, Block contradicts the common view that Hopper is a narrative painter. Instead, he argues that his paintings do not tell stories, but that they suggest 'that there are stories within them waiting to be told'.[26] Hopper portrays a moment in time in each of his paintings and he leaves it to the viewer to uncover the past and the future of that moment and find a story within it. Block engaged sixteen authors to write a picture's story and concluded the collection with one of his own. Some of the stories 'spring directly from the canvas', suggesting that the author has written the story to fit the painting, whilst others 'rebound at an oblique angle from the canvas', triggering a story the picture has inspired within the author. Block identifies only two common denominators to the stories in the collection: excellence and their source in one of Hopper's paintings. However, many of the stories share other features. Most of them are period pieces, with only one, Jonathan Santlofer's 'Night Windows', set in the age in which the story was written, rather than that in which the painting was made. None of the stories based on Hopper's art is cheerful, but they do plumb the depths. Be warned: many are bitter tales with sick jokes and violent sex.

When the writer keeps a close eye on the painting as the story is told, the reader can be led around the artwork to observe otherwise unobtrusive detail. This is why, when I read the stories, I kept a finger in the page showing the paintings and often flicked back and forth between picture and text. Warren Moore's 'Office at Night', inspired by Hopper's 1940 painting of the same title, tells the story of an office manager, Walter, engaging a new secretary. Moore notices the cord of the window shade blowing in the breeze from the open window, the light from the window shining on the wall and the desk light illuminating the papers Walter is reading. Without Moore to guide us, however, we might not notice the sheet of paper that has fluttered to the floor either from the filing cabinet drawer the new secretary is leaning against or from Walter's desk. Similarly, without Stephen King to guide us in his story, 'The Music Room', we might not notice that the young woman at the piano in Hopper's *Room in New York* (1932) is merely stroking the keys and not playing it. Other stories imagine what cannot be seen in the painting, either because, as in

---

26. Ibid., p. viii.

Hopper's *Night Windows* (1928), depicting a woman only partially visible through three windows, the scene is incomplete or because the writer imagines for the sake of his or her story something off stage: Lee Child's 'The Truth about What Happened', inspired by the 1943 painting entitled *Hotel Lobby*, imagines rooms beyond the door Hopper depicts and imagines features not depicted in the painting, such as a lobby and a reception desk that one would reasonably expect to be there. Block's own 'Autumn at the Automat', inspired by Hopper's *Automat* (1927), also refers to an alligator handbag that the solitary woman in the painting does not have, other tables with solitary diners that must be off stage, staff employed by the diner and an exit door.

In almost every instance, Hopper's art is an exploration of isolation and solitariness, encapsulating in paint the yearning of the American dream. In *Nighthawks* (1942) the artist observes three customers and a server in a diner from outside at night. There is little sign of human interaction among the human figures in the painting. In *Hotel by a Railroad* (1952), the woman reads a book while the man, cigarette in hand, looks out of the window. In *Summer Evening* (1947), a young couple may be sharing a quiet and reflective conversation or simply an intimate time of peaceful quiet as they lean against the railing of a veranda, but even they are isolated, surrounded by the black of night. Much more common in Hopper's work are depictions of solitary figures: the young woman in the automat, the naked woman standing in the sun of her bedroom in *A Woman in the Sun* (1961), another naked woman sitting in a blue chair by a window in *Eleven A.M.* painted in 1926, a cinema usherette in *New York Movie* (1939), a woman sitting on her bed reading in *Hotel Room* painted in 1931 and many more. These invite viewers to ask why they are alone: what is their story?

Most of the stories in Block's collection self-consciously refer to Hopper, but none more specifically than Gail Levin's 'The Preacher Collects'. Levin was both Hopper's biographer and editor of his catalogue of work. Her story rests on Doris Lessing's premise, which Levin quotes in her introduction, that 'fiction is better at "the truth" than a factual record',[27] and is inspired by Hopper's *City Roofs* of 1932. It tells the story of an actual minister, Arthayer R. Sanborn, who, disappointed by the pittance he was paid for officiating at

---

27. Ibid., p. 155.

Hopper's funeral in 1967, claimed that Hopper's widow had given him an unsold canvas called *City Roofs*. According to Levin, Sanborn had 'adopted' it. He had also acquired a suitcase full of Hopper's early works which he had salvaged from Hopper's attic when no one else was interested in them. Levin discovered these discrepancies when she was curating exhibitions of Hopper's art at the Whitney Museum on two occasions in 1979 and 1980, and she uses the story to establish her view that Sanborn was not entitled to these artworks. Whereas he believed he was collecting on a debt for services rendered, for which he felt he had been paid too little, Levin's accusation, made in the form of fiction, is that he had, in fact, stolen them.

One other story in the collection also features a church minister: Craig Ferguson's 'Taking Care of Business', inspired by *South Truro Church* (1930), which depicts a solitary, quite plain church set against an evening sky. The shadows are long. Ferguson describes the sky as 'cold and still with a high milky cataract of cloud diffusing the sunlight enough to flatter the landscape'.[28] The story he weaves from the picture is that of the Reverend Jefferson T. Adams, a long-serving and much-loved minister, who shares two secrets with a friend he has known for over 70 years. The first is that, as a child, he was adopted. In the absence of records of his birth, his adoptive parents spin the outrageous tale that he was Elvis Presley's twin, sold by parents who had feared they could not afford to support two babies. The second secret is that he is an atheist. Years of ministry have driven belief out of him, yet he had continued to preach about God because he 'was just taking care of the family business'.[29] The solitary, closed up church in the picture inspires Ferguson to imagine a secretive, isolated character, cast adrift from his natural parents and set apart from others in the clerical profession as a non-believer. The stark appearance of the building matches the interior bleakness of Jefferson Adams.

It seems to me that in many respects what these, and other, writers are doing in response to visual art is related to Simone Weil's spirituality of waiting on God. Earlier I said that she regarded all concentrated occupation – learning a language, riding a bike or conducting an experiment – as a form of contemplation, but that this

---

28. Ibid., p. 107.
29. Ibid., p. 113.

concentration need not be intentional. One can ride a bike naturally, concentrating instinctively rather than intentionally.[30] When touring an art gallery, attending a performance of a symphony, going to a music festival, watching a film in the cinema, or participating in any artistic endeavour, we might catch a glimpse of the divine at any unexpected moment. Yet, we can make it intentional. It can it become an intentional spiritual exercise from which we might benefit and by which the soul can be fed, enriching life.

I offer three ideas, which can nourish you spiritually, for you to consider when reading. First, ekphrasis relies on close observation. We have seen above that poets and short story writers begin by looking closely at a work of art, noting details that cursory glances might miss. In some instances, they keep their detailed observations in their writing, meaning that the reader does not need to see the picture, but often they leave their observational notes behind when they write. Even then the writing would be impossible without the prior looking. Simply standing and staring at a work of art, immersing oneself in a film or being absorbed in a symphony is spiritually uplifting. Close reading of a text can also touch our spiritual being, as we linger over a word or phrase, enjoy the structure of a sentence or become immersed in the arc of a narrative. Try reading John Clare's deeply moving poem, 'I am – yet what I am none cares or knows', for instance, lingering over each word and phrase, and see whether you can avoid 'abid[ing] with [your] Creator God' by the time you have spent some minutes with it. Then will you not find yourself being where Clare longs to be 'Untroubling and untroubled … The grass below – above the vaulted sky'?

Second, your reading can be fuel for your spiritual journey if you practise writing a journal. Keeping a journal is a well-trodden spiritual exercise. As an aspect of spiritual direction, the person under direction often keeps an online blog or a private diary recording feelings, experiences and thoughts. The journal can be enhanced by reflections on, and insights from, what one has read and can be most productive if this has begun with close attention to the text.

Third, as an alternative to keeping a journal, try a creative writing exercise such as writing a story based on what you have read, in the way Block's collection of authors wove stories around the Hopper

---

30. See Williams, *Luminaries*, p. 128.

paintings they studied. What story do you find in Clare's 'I am'? Perhaps a better way to express this question is to ask: what story does Clare's 'I am' inspire within you? By the time you have completed the story, your self-understanding has developed as much as your engagement with the poem has, and, more importantly, you have moved deeper into God and understood better God's ways with you.

10

Escaping the Net

The publication of Iris Murdoch's debut novel, *Under the Net* (1954), announced the arrival on the literary scene of a bold and brilliant novelist, to whose work I turn time and again. Murdoch dedicated her creative life to writing fiction, but her academic life was as a philosopher. She wrestled with her dual vocation because she was convinced that there was a fundamental disjunction between the two disciplines. Whereas philosophy 'states and attempts to solve very difficult, highly technical problems … art is fun', she said, 'and for fun, it has innumerable intentions and charms'.[1] In my view, theology is a branch of philosophy, although not all philosophers are theologians. I have often said that a similar tension exists between theology and literature: theology tends to want to systematise and reach conclusions and agreed statements, whilst literature is content to live with paradox and unresolved difference.

Under the Net was Murdoch's first literary foray into the debate that was to occupy all her working life: what has philosophy to do with literature? Our concern in this book is related to this. What has theology to do with fiction? Can reading feed a person's religious appetite? Can reading satisfy spiritual yearning? Can it quench the thirst for meaning and fulfil the quest for purpose?

Two contemporary novelists, each with quite different perspectives, give us the impression that the distance between theology and

---

1. Quoted by Kieran Setiya, 'Frivolous and Profound: Philosophy, Fiction and Fun', *Times Literary Supplement*, 8 September 2023, p. 27.

literature is so great that there is little hope of one relating to the other. In 2004, Philip Pullman argued that there is a fundamental and insurmountable disjunction between religious and literary minds. He argued that reading is a democratic activity, while religion, with its natural inclination towards establishing dogma, will always tend towards discouraging freedom of thought.[2] In the following year, Chimamanda Ngozi Adichie expressed her opinion that very low, almost negligible, sales of fiction throughout her native Nigeria were the result of fundamentalist forms of both Islam and Christianity setting out to suppress all nuanced thinking. She argued that these forms of religion excluded subtlety from Nigerian public life.[3] Both Pullman and Adichie discern current instances of religion's hostility towards fiction which repeat earlier cases of religious antagonism towards fiction, to which I referred in Chapter Three. However, the disjunction is not essential.

Indeed, the recurring debate among those who research in the field of Christianity and the arts is whether the arts are mere handmaidens of theology or profoundly theological in their nature? For instance, does a painting of the Annunciation merely illustrate an aspect of the doctrine of Incarnation or is it capable of contributing to its theology? In the case of the literary arts, do fiction and poetry create and develop theology, or merely illustrate it? I have learnt over many years of reading theologically that, because literature tolerates paradox and resists any reductive tendencies, literature can 'contain the faith'. Secular written works can express and help define what it is we believe and what it means to believe. This was hinted at in Francis Pott's hymn of the Victorian era in which the worshippers join their voices with those of the angels and sing that 'craftsman's art and music's measure for [God's] pleasure all combine'.[4] Here the 'craftsman's art' includes the literary arts.

The contention of this book is that fiction is capable of carrying, expressing and bolstering religious faith, and its intention is to encourage Christians to read widely in their quest for deeper understanding of God. In short, we are reaching for a spirituality of

---

2. Philip Pullman, 'The War on Words', *The Guardian*, 6 November 2004.
3. Chimamanda Ngozi Adichie 'Blinded by God's Business', *The Guardian*, 19 February 2005.
4. 'Angel Voices, Ever Singing' (1861) in many hymnbooks.

reading through which literature feeds the soul. Murdoch's *Under the Net* demonstrates this.

Under the Net begins when Jake Donaghue, who describes himself as a professional 'unauthorised person' and who earns his money as a translator, is kicked out of the flat he was sharing with his quasi-girlfriend, the woman to whom it belongs. This sets in train a series of picaresque adventures as he drifts from place to place. His travels after eviction are a mixture of flight from mature responsibility and a serious quest for meaning and purpose: 'Jake capers through the streets of London, chases a lost love to Paris, kidnaps a showbiz dog, breaks an estranged friend out of a head-injury ward, picks locks, gambles, drinks, does judo and is self-deceived.'[5] In the convention of the picaresque novel, Jake tells his own story and admits to being riven with envy when he discovers that the (in his eyes) second-rate French novelist whom he translates for a living has been awarded the Prix Goncourt. Now he sees this novelist, Breteuil, no longer as a business partner but as a rival. In his recent article for the *Times Literary Supplement*, Setiya asks whether *Under the Net* is the novel this rivalry inspired him (Jake) to write; for Setiya sees Jake Donaghue as the author of *Under the Net* as much as Iris Murdoch. Is he a stand-in for Murdoch as she struggles with the lack of common ground between philosophy and literature?

It is well-known that Murdoch resented readings of her novels as 'philosophy-in-disguise',[6] but despite its light-heartedness, it cannot be denied that *Under the Net* is deeply involved with philosophical ideas. In his comments on the novel, Setiya says it is 'undeniably philosophical'. The novel is dedicated to Raymond Queneau and its central conversation between Jake and Hugo in the cold-cure centre, which Jake decides to write up as 'The Silencer' without crediting Hugo, includes ideas about language that are not far removed from those of Wittgenstein. Jake had been ashamed of 'The Silencer', and regarded it as juvenile and derivative. Indeed, most of it was what Hugo had said, and yet, when he looks at it again after he has sprung Hugo from hospital, he is surprised to find it more original than he had thought. Jake's philosophical essay has an important role in the novel in setting out its central problem. Because Jake has written two

---

5. Setiya, 'Frivolous and Profound'.
6. Peter J. Conradi, *The Saint and the Artist: A Study of the Fiction of Iris Murdoch* (London: Harper Collins, 1989), p. 38.

books – 'The Silencer', a philosophical conversation, and Murdoch's *Under the Net* – readers find that Murdoch is posing a fundamental question: what can fiction do that philosophy cannot do? Or, more specifically for readers interested in the spirituality of novels, what can fiction do that theology, as a branch of philosophy, cannot do? There are some tentative answers in *Under the Net*.

First, in the conversation Jake has with Hugo in the cold-cure centre, Jake thinks he gets to the heart of Hugo's mindset during a discussion of Proust when they touched on what it meant to describe a feeling or a state of mind. It was clear that the concept puzzled Hugo, who commented that there was 'something fishy about describing people's feelings'. They were usually described so dramatically that they are 'falsified from the start'.[7] The description cannot be true, he says, despite the noblest of efforts to achieve accuracy. Because descriptions of feelings or states of mind are given retrospectively, Hugo argues that the time lapse and the time for reflection compromise the accuracy of the description. Almost everything one says, he agrees, 'turns out to be a sort of lie'.[8] The implication of this conversation is that descriptions of emotion do have their proper place in novels. Without discussion of characters' feelings, motives or state of mind, fiction would be dull and something of a spent force. Of course, Hugo's philosophical stance is overstated here, but it does draw our attention to an important distinction between the disciplines: fiction, among other things, is to do with the internal, emotions and feelings, whilst philosophy deals with 'hard science'.

The title, *Under the Net*, suggests physical confinement, rather than the freedom Jake seems to enjoy once he has been evicted. He is now as free to roam as Don Quixote! Nevertheless, there are several symbolic scenes of enclosure and imprisonment throughout the novel. The cold-cure centre holds people, sometimes in solitary confinement, for a fortnight to assess their reaction to possible cold cures. The mime theatre at night, including Anna's untidy office, is an eerie, cluttered and restricted space: speech is rare and the silence is filled with strange noises. In another episode, Jake is locked in Sadie's flat and escapes only by some hilarious means. When we first meet the showbiz dog, Mister Mars, he is trapped in a cage and the only way Jake can kidnap him is to take the cage. In the head-injury

---

7. Iris Murdoch, *Under the Net* (London: Vintage Books, 2002), p. 66.
8. Ibid., p. 67.

hospital, Hugo was concussed, his head is bandaged and he cannot leave his bed without assistance. None of these traps are, however, the net of which the title speaks. The extract from 'The Silencer' that Jake reads refers to this net: he writes, 'All theorizing is flight. We must be ruled by the situation itself and this is unutterably particular. Indeed it is something to which we can never get close enough, however hard we may try as it were to crawl under the net.'[9] In interview, years after the publication of Under the Net, Murdoch identified the net as the net of language. Peter Conradi narrows down the reference even further to Wittgenstein's Tractatus 6.341 which speaks of 'the net of discourse behind which the world's particularities hide'.[10] Language is necessary to elicit and describe whatever is around and within us; but language can also be employed to hide what we do not want to expose. In the extract from 'The Silencer', Hugo, in the form of Jake's invented interlocutor, Annandine, says that he would therefore eschew language because 'for most of us, truth can only be attained, if at all, only in silence. It is in silence that the human spirit touches the divine'.[11] Only towards the end of the novel, when all the words have been spoken, are Hugo and Jake able to crawl from under the net of language's limitations and move into the silence of understanding.[12]

Jake, as the fictitious author of Under the Net, demonstrates artifice as a storyteller, yet he is unable either to understand or communicate to us the nature of his relationship with Hugo. Moreover, he is dependent upon Hugo's account of events to help him make sense of his own rather messy life. Novels are always polyvocal; they have more than one voice. In addition to that of author and narrator, readers hear the voices of their characters. In all its inventiveness and fun, its many intentions and charms (to use Murdoch's own phrase), in all its many voices, fiction reaches for truthfulness. Fiction's essential shapeshifting characteristic enables fiction to speak more truthfully. Yet Under the Net's conclusion is that 'Actions don't lie, words always do.'[13] At its very end, Jake looks at a litter of newborn kittens and puzzles over how genetics works, because he finds he is unable to explain why some are Siamese in appearance and others are not. He

---

9. Ibid., p. 91.
10. Conradi, The Saint and the Artist, p. 40.
11. Murdoch, Under the Net, p. 92.
12. Hilda D. Spear, Iris Murdoch (London: Macmillan, 1995), pp. 21-22.
13. Murdoch, Under the Net, p. 257.

does not have the language to explain, and this concluding episode, like the rest of the novel, problematises language as a bearer of true narrative. Nevertheless, instead of writing tomes of philosophy to explain, Jake chooses to write the novel we are reading.

He chooses to write *Under the Net* because fiction can deal seriously with ephemeral experience and treat experience of the divine lightly. The story Jake tells is light-hearted, at times flippant, and often amusing, yet it describes a serious quest for truth and understanding. He writes:

> What is urgent is not urgent forever but only ephemerally. All work and all love, the search for wealth and fame, the search for truth, life itself, are made up of moments which pass and become nothing. Yet through this shaft of nothings we drive onward with that miraculous vitality that creates our precarious habitations in the past and the future. So we live.[14]

Peter Conradi says that these narratives can be the pompous musings of a fool or the deepest truth words can register; and I say that this ambivalence exists because this is fiction, not philosophy. It is fiction's plurality of vision that enables novels to have a helpfully ambiguous relationship with life's various truths. Or, as Conradi expressed it, 'Good art is philosophy swimming, or philosophy drowning.'[15] Good art is theology both swimming and drowning.

According to Cottingham, Augustine and many philosophers in the centuries since have all seen that 'it is of the nature of a finite creature to reach towards the infinite – something it cannot fully grasp, but which it somehow apprehends even in the very awareness of its own finitude'.[16] This is the essence of what it means to be a spiritual being, a reaching beyond oneself to a higher reality. Matthew Arnold famously concluded in the later years of the nineteenth century that religion is on the ebb, saying that '[t]here is not a creed which is not shaken, not an accredited dogma which is not shown to be questionable, not a received tradition which does not threaten to dissolve'. He suggested that the vacuum being left by fading religion is filled with poetry and

---

14. Ibid., p. 275.
15. Conradi, *The Saint and the Artist*, p. 38.
16. Cottingham, *In Search of the Soul*, p. 133.

that literature will carry the future.[17] I hope there will always be a place for good religion in human society, and I believe there will be a role for literature within that future. Unlike Arnold, I do not think that literature will replace religion, but that each will be a mutually moderating influence on the other. They will exist side by side in mutual compatibility. Literature, especially literary fiction with its focus on narrative, character and ideas, will challenge instances of unwarranted religious assertiveness, and will stimulate readers' natural spiritual tendencies and lift them in their quest for the infinite and ineffable. Literature is capable of speaking of God because God's voice may be one of a novel's many voices. Religion's perpetual implication that there is more to life than meets the eye will uplift even those novels with mundane anti-transcendental tendencies.

In *Middlemarch*, George Eliot's Dorothea fears that Casaubon is so ill that he will not recover and she asks Dr Lydgate for his prognosis. She beseeches the doctor to speak plainly. Lydgate explains that Casaubon's case is one on which it is difficult to pronounce. He may live for another fifteen years in reasonable health if he is careful and rests, or he may not. Dorothea thanks him for his candour. For years after, Lydgate remembers this conversation as 'a cry from soul to soul'.[18] The act of reading is a cry from soul to soul, as we engage with characters in realist fiction, as we absorb ourselves in the magical realism of fantasy in fiction, as we converse with fiction's authors. In all these, we are reaching for the numinous beyond us and questing for the true self. Fictional characters' experiences can trigger something that can help us deal with our own experiences. For this reason, Josie Billington decries the modern habit of quick scanning or light reading, because it silences the text's voices and thoughts. Careful and caring reading, which does not know its own aims or purposes in advance, but lets the text speak on its own terms, which can also be known as charitable reading, 'energizes what is otherwise kept enfolded within books and latent inside people'.[19] As an example of this liberating effect of what she called 'real reading', Billington cites the well-known example of Jeanette Winterson, who 'found in all the great works of literature "a tough language" to support a tough

---

17. Cited in Edmundson, *Why Read?*, p. 136.
18. George Eliot, *Middlemarch* (Harmondsworth: Penguin, 1965), p. 324.
19. Billington, *Is Literature Healthy?*, p. 135.

and damaged life'.[20] Winterson escaped the religious fundamentalism of her adoptive mother through reading. Billington had asked whether literature is healthy, whether reading is good for you. At the end of her exploration of the question, she commented that health is having the space and a place to think everything and anything, and it struck me, as I read her conclusion, that this is not far from my understanding of the relationship between theology and literature. Over the years as a reader, both as a student of literature and a theologian, I have found that doing theology through literature gives me space to think anything and thus to grow spiritually as I read. Literature provides precious space in this fast world for slow thinking. Such slow thinking, I find, raises our awareness of the divine.

One of the most daring twenty-first-century novelists, because of the extent to which he explores the nature of religious belief and because he sets so much of his work in ecclesial settings, is Michael Arditti. His *Jubilate* is set in Lourdes while a television crew prepare a documentary about a group of pilgrims. Among them is a married couple, Gillian and Richard. A brain trauma some years previously had reduced Richard to a child-like state in which he had lost most social inhibitions. Both his mother and wife accompany Richard on the pilgrimage, his mother a true believer who prays for a miracle, and his wife much more sceptical. In one scene Richard's mother tries to persuade him to visit the Grotto. He refuses on the basis that it is grotty. Overhearing this exchange, one of the attendant priests, Father Dave, interjects, saying that it used to be grotty but that does not explain why it is called a grotto. In fact, he says, it used to be the town's rubbish dump and it became a sacred site because Bernadette looked there for wood. 'What does that tell us today?' Father Dave asks. 'How would I know?' Richard responds tetchily. When the priests offers an answer to his own question, that because God is everywhere we can find God in the most unexpected places, the uninhibited Richard offers a child-like truth when he asks, '[Unexpected places] like toilets?'[21] Father Dave is forced to agree. This scene illustrates in a light-hearted, humorous way the basis on which this spirituality of reading has been constructed, which is that we can meet God anywhere and everywhere; we can encounter God, not only in sacred scriptures but in all reading and writing. Reading feeds the soul, and,

---

20. Ibid., p. 112.
21. Michael Arditti, *Jubilate* (London: Arcadia, 2011), p. 229.

for this reason, this book aims to encourage people of faith to read widely and roam free in the world of literature.

The liberation of reading, imagining ourselves out of our prisons of self-regard and transience, crawling from under the net to dream ourselves into the world outside and beyond us, brings us to a point of thanksgiving, which, according to John Donne, as we noted towards the end of Chapter Seven, is the purest form of prayer. Reading becomes something for which we are grateful, and such grateful reading is, I suggest, a high form of spirituality in which the transcended self is both lost and found in the divine. Through reaching towards the infinite in reading, we may escape the prison of ephemerality, mortality and mundanity, just as young David Copperfield escaped to that room containing his father's books and found there a safe place that was a lifesaver for him. I have sought to demonstrate that a lifetime of reading literature, especially poetry and novels of ideas, rescues us also, by helping us form our true selves and by drawing us closer to God, in whose image we are made.

Bibliography

Adichie, Chimamanda Ngozi 'Blinded by God's Business', *The Guardian*, 19 February 2005
Allan, Nina, 'Cuddy by Benjamin Myers Review: A Visionary History', *The Guardian*, 9 March 2023
Augustine of Hippo, *Confessions* (Harmondsworth: Penguin Classics, 1961)
Billington, Josie, *Is Literature Healthy?* (Oxford: Oxford University Press, 2016)
Block, Lawrence, ed., *In Sunlight or in Shadow: Stories Inspired by the Paintings of Edward Hopper* (New York, NY: Pegasus Books, 2016)
Carson, Ciaran, *Still Life* (Salem, MA: Wake Forest University Press, 2020)
Chadwick, Henry, *Augustine of Hippo: A Life* (Oxford: Oxford University Press, 2009)
Coleman, Daniel, *In Bed with the Word: Reading, Spirituality, and Cultural Politics* (Edmonton: University of Alberta Press, 2009)
Collins, Deborah, *Thomas Hardy and His God: A Liturgy of Unbelief* (New York, NY: St Martin's Press, 1990)
Conradi, Peter J., *The Saint and the Artist: A Study of the Fiction of Iris Murdoch* (London: Harper Collins, 1989)
Cottingham, John, *In Search of the Soul: A Philosophical Essay* (Princeton, NJ: Princeton University Press, 2020)
Cupitt, Don, *Mysticism after Modernity* (Oxford: Blackwell, 1998)
Davis, Philip, *Reading for Life* (Oxford: Oxford University Press, 2020)
Dickens, Charles, *David Copperfield* (Ware: Wordsworth Classics, 1992)
Dickens, Charles, *Hard Times* (Harmondsworth: Penguin Classics, 1995)
Dickinson, David, *Yet Alive? Methodists in British Fiction since 1890* (Newcastle upon Tyne: Cambridge Scholars Publishing, 2016)
Drury, John, *Music at Midnight: The Life and Poetry of George Herbert* (London: Allen Lane, 2013)
Dumitrescu, Irina, 'Eating Their Words', *Times Literary Supplement*, 30 September 2022
Edmundson, Mark, *Why Read?* (New York, NY: Bloomsbury, 2004)

Eliot, George, *Middlemarch* (Harmondsworth: Penguin, 1965)
Faulks, Sebastian, *Faulks on Fiction: The Secret Life of the Novel* (London: BBC Books, 2011)
Fiddes, Paul, ed., *The Novel, Spirituality and Modern Culture* (Cardiff: University of Wales Press, 2000)
Fischer, Steven Roger, *A History of Reading* (London: Reaktion Books, 2003)
Forster, E.M., *A Passage to India* (Harmondsworth: Penguin Modern Classics, 1961)
Furbank, P.N., *E.M. Forster: A Life*, 2 vols (London: Secker & Warburg, 1977-78)
Gill, Theodore, ed., *The Sermons of John Donne* (New York, NY: Meridian Books, 1958)
Greening, John, 'Review of Maitreyabandhu, *After Cézanne*', *Times Literary Supplement*, 21 March 2020
Harries, Richard, *Art and the Beauty of God: A Christian Understanding* (London: Mowbray, 1993)
Herbst, Matthew T., '"The Pernicious Effects of Novel Reading": The Methodist Episcopal Campaign against American Fiction 1865-1914', *Journal of Religion and Society* 9 (2007), pp. 1-15
Jacobs, Alan, *A Theology of Reading: The Hermeneutics of Love* (Boulder, CO: Westview Press, 2001)
Jeffrey, David Lyle, *People of the Book: Christian Identity and Literary Culture* (Grand Rapids, MI: William B. Eerdmans, 1996)
Jenkins, Nicholas, 'Historical as Munich: Auden at 100: Who Is He Now?', *Times Literary Supplement*, 9 February 2007
Kirsch, Arthur, *Auden and Christianity* (New Haven, CT: Yale University Press, 2005)
Kramnick, Jonathan, *Criticism and Truth: On Method in Literary Studies* (Chicago: The University of Chicago Press, 2023)
Leighton, Angela, *On Form: Poetry, Aestheticism, and the Legacy of a Word* (Oxford: Oxford University Press, 2007)
Loughlin, Gerard, 'The Man Who Fell to Earth', in *The Blackwell Companion to Postmodern Theology*, edited by Graham Ward (Oxford: Blackwell, 2001), pp. 24-47
Lowry, Elizabeth, 'Listening for the Echo: Re-reading A Passage to India', *Times Literary Supplement*, 5 June 2020
Maitreyabandhu, *After Cézanne* (Hexham: Bloodaxe Books, 2019)
Malone, Nancy M., *Walking a Literary Labyrinth: A Spirituality of Reading* (New York, NY: Riverhead Books, 2003)
Marno, David, *Death Be Not Proud: The Art of Holy Attention* (Chicago: University of Chicago Press, 2016)
Mawer, Simon, *The Fall* (London: Little, Brown, 2003)

Bibliography

Mumford, James, 'Biblical Reverses: How Thomas Hardy Plotted against God', *Times Literary Supplement*, 3 May 2019, pp. 4-5

Murdoch, Iris, *Under the Net* (London: Vintage Classics, 2002)

Murdoch, Iris, *The Unicorn* (London: Chatto & Windus, 1963)

Myers, Benjamin, *Cuddy* (London: Bloomsbury, 2023)

Perraudin, Frances, 'Bard Labour: Boost Workplace Productivity "by Reading a Poem"', *The Guardian*, 6 March 2020

Phillips, D.Z., *R.S. Thomas: Poet of the Hidden God: Meaning and Mediation in the Poetry of RS Thomas* (London: Macmillan, 1986)

Prickett, Stephen, ed., *The Edinburgh Companion to the Bible and the Arts* (Edinburgh: Edinburgh University Press, 2014)

Pullman, Philip, 'The War on Words', *The Guardian*, 6 November 2004

Radcliffe, Timothy, *Alive in God: A Christian Imagination* (London: Bloomsbury, 2019)

Riggle, Nick, *This Beauty: A Philosophy of Being Alive* (London: Hachette, 2022)

Robertson, James, *The Testament of Gideon Mack* (London: Penguin, 2006)

Robinson-Brown, Jarel, 'Living in the Monotony of Prayer', Modern Church website; available online at: https://modernchurch.org.uk/jarel-robinson-brown-living-in-the-monotony-of-prayer (accessed 13 July 2024)

Rodd, C.S., 'God and the Novelists: 9. Thomas Hardy', *Expository Times* 110, no. 7 (1999), pp. 205-9

Royle, Nicholas, *E.M. Forster* (Plymouth: Northcote House, 1999)

Sells, Michael, *Mystical Languages of Unsaying* (Chicago: University of Chicago Press, 1994)

Setiya, Kieran, 'Frivolous and Profound: Philosophy, Fiction and Fun', *Times Literary Supplement*, 8 September 2023

Setiya, Kieran, 'The Line of Beauty: Why We're Glad to Be Alive', *Times Literary Supplement*, 18 November 2022

Shafak, Elif, *Three Daughters of Eve* (New York, NY: Bloomsbury, 2016)

Sheldrake, Philip, ed., *Heaven in Ordinary: George Herbert and His Writings* (Norwich: Canterbury Press, 2009)

Smith, Emma, *Portable Magic: A History of Books and Their Readers* (London: Allen Lane, 2022)

Spear, Hilda D., *Iris Murdoch* (London: Macmillan, 1995)

Spring, Marion, *Howard* (London: Collins, 1967)

Stock, Brian, *Augustine the Reader: Meditation, Self-Knowledge, and the Ethics of Interpretation* (Cambridge MA: Harvard University Press, 1996)

Taylor, Helen, *Why Women Read Fiction: The Stories of Our Lives* (Oxford: Oxford University Press, 2019)

Thomas, R.S., *Between Here and Now* (London: Macmillan, 1981)

Thomas, R.S., *Collected Poems: 1945-1990* (London: J.M. Dent, 1993)
Williams, J.P., *Seeking the God Beyond: A Beginner's Guide to Christian Apophatic Spirituality* (London: SCM Press, 2018)
Williams, Rowan, *Luminaries: Twenty Lives that Illuminate the Christian Way* (London: SPCK, 2019)
Winterson, Jeanette, *Why Be Happy When You Could Be Normal?* (London: Vintage, 2011)

Index

absent characters 76
Adichie, Chimamanda Ngozi 140
Allington, Cyril 117-8
Apophatic 72-5
Arcimboldo, Giuseppe 69
Arditti, Michael 146
Aristotle 44
Armstrong, Karen 75-6
Aquinas 100
Arnold, Matthew 128, 144-5
Attentiveness 35, 86, 99
Auden, WH.
    Musée des Beaux Arts 131-3
    September 1, 1939 87-9
Augustine
    Confessions 9-10, 31
    De doctrina Christiana 31
    De Musica 15
    De quantitate animae 17-18
    De Trinitate 20-21, 76
    Education 13-14
    Fall 14
    literary output 13
    mystical experiences 10-11
    Ostia 11-12
    silent reading 14-15
    sound and silence 15-16

Banks, Iain 42-43
Barth, Karl 71
Barthes, Roland 104-5
Basil the Great 34
beauty 103, 106-7, 117
Bible
    Exodus 15:25 16
    Exodus 33:7 3
    Psalm 19:10 38
    Psalm 62:11 65
    Psalm 86:1 67
    Isaiah 61: 1-2 61
    Ezekiel 3:3 38
    Luke 15:11-32 39-40, 68
    Acts 17:28 28
    1 Corinthians 9:9 17
    1 Corinthians 15:33 28
    Titus 1:15 27
Bibliolatry 45
Blake, William 109-110
Block, Lawrence 133-6
Book of Common Prayer 38
books as neighbours 28-29
Bunyan, John 64

Cataphatic 72
Cezanne, Paul 120, 121-5

Einstein's Watch 122-3
Man with a Pipe 122
Mme Cezanne in Blue 123-4
Self-Portrait with a Beret 125
The Blue Vase 124-5
Three Skulls on an Oriental Rug 125
Clare, John 137-8
close reading 85, 137
Cosnett, Elizabeth 72
Crane, Stephen 26-27

Dearmer, Percy 102
Defoe, Daniel 5
Desert Island Discs 66
Detroit Conference of the Methodist
   Episcopal Church 24-5
deus absconditus 131
Dickens, Charles
   A Christmas Carol 65
   David Copperfield 1-2, 147
   Great Expectations 63
   Hard Times 2
Dickinson, Emily 4
Donne, John 100-1, 147
   Death Be Not Proud 98
Duffy, Carol Ann 93-7
Dumitrescu, Irina 38-9

eating texts 38
Eckhart, Meister 74
ekphrasis 119ff.
Eliot, George 30-1
   Middlemarch 77, 145
Emerson, Ralph Waldo 51
Eriugena, John Scotus 74
Evaristo, Bernardine 16

fish and turtle legend 73
form 103-5, 110-111
Forster, EM

A Passage to India 77-84
Aspects of the Novel 81

Gill, Eric 30
Goethe, Johann 33
Gregory of Nyssa 72

Hardy, Thomas 53-60, 81-2
Herbert, George
   The Bag 92
   The Elixir 13, 129
   Prayer (I) 89-93
hermeneutics of suspicion 47-8
Hocking, Josiah, Silas and Salome 26
holy attention 86, 99
home 108
Hopper, Edward 133-6
Howells, HD 27
humans as spiritual beings 7-8

imagination 46
inspiration 18-19

James, Henry 106-7
Jefferson, Thomas 25
Jerome 27-8
journal 137
Joyce, James 15

Keats, John 106-7, 120-1

labyrinth 125-7

Maitreyabandhu 121-6
Malebranche, Nicolas 98-9, 101
Mawer, Simon 40-42
McGough, Roger 119
meaning, figurative and literal 16-17
memory 18
Michigan Christian Advocate 24

Index

Middleton, Stanley 22
Milton, John 108
Montgomery, James 97-8
Murdoch, Iris
    The Unicorn 39, 62
    Under the Net 139, 140-144
Myers, Benjamin 112-7

National Literary Trust 21
New Criticism 29-30
New York Times 119
Nimoy, Leonard 102
nothingness 82-3

order 108-9

parable of the prodigal son 39-40, 68
Peterson, Don 119
Plotinus 19
Porete, Marguerite 74
Potts, Francis 140
prayer and thinking 98-99
Pseudo-Dionysius 94
Pullman, Philip 140

reading
    charitable 30ff.
    kenotic 62
    quixotic 64
    real 145
reading as a spiritual exercise 13
Reading for Life project 62
reading habits 6
Ricoeur, Paul 47-8
Robertson, James 35-37
Rolle, Richard 28

Schopenhauer 62
self-conscious reader 19-20

Shafak, Elif 108
Shared Reading programme 48-51
silence 81
Sinclair, Upton 26-7
Solomon and Saturn I 38
spirituality
    definition 6-7
    and individuality 8
spiritual practice 9
Spring, Howard 25
stages of reading 20

Talmud 30
Teresa of Avila 51-2, 64
Tertullian 27
thinking as prayer 98-9, 101
Thomas, RS.75, 126-130
    Degas: Woman Ironing 129-130
    Gauguin: The Alyscamps at Arles 129
    Pisarro: Landscape at Chaponval 128
    The Church at Auvers 129
    The Other 128
    Threshold 126-7
    Van Gogh: Portrait of Dr Gachet 130
time, consciousness of 17-18
Tucker, Charlotte Maria (A.L.O.E) 26
via affirmativa 72
via negativa 2
Victoria and Albert Museum 71

Weatherhead, Leslie 25
Weil, Simone 86, 136-7
Wesley, John 68
will 18
Winterson, Jeanette 26, 145-6
Wittgenstein 143

You may also be interested in:
Make-Believe

God in 21st Century Novels
David Dickinson

"I will tell you a story that will make you believe in God."
No story can guarantee being able to do this. Yet novelists can tell stories that make us think about what we believe about God and why.

Despite repeated predictions of the death of the novel, thousands of works of fiction are published and read in Britain each year. Although Western society is less religiously observant than it was, many 21st-century novelists persist in pursuing theological, religious and spiritual themes. Make-Believe seeks to explain why.

With chapters offering analyses of novels from several genres – so-called literary fiction, historical fiction, science fiction, fantasy and dystopia – David Dickinson discusses a wide spectrum of novelists. Authors who are avowedly atheistic and authors who have a vested interest in perpetuating biblical stories are both featured. Well-known writers such as Rushdie, McEwan, McCarthy and Martell rub shoulders with some you may be meeting for the first time. Appealing to literature students and people who simply enjoy reading, whether Christian or not, this study of God in novels invites us to open our minds and allow aspects of our culture to shape our understanding of God and to change our ways of talking about the divine.

David Dickinson taught secondary school English in Newcastle upon Tyne before training for the Methodist ministry. He has researched and written in the field of theology and literature since the early 1990s and ministered in churches since the late 1980s. His publications include *The Novel as Church* (2013) and *Yet Alive? Methodists in British Fiction since 1890* (2016).

Published 2020

Paperback ISBN: 978 0 7188 9547 1
ePub ISBN: 978 0 7188 4800 2
PDF ISBN: 978 0 7188 4799 9

You may also be interested in:
Literature and Religion
A Dialogue Between China and the West
David Jasper and Ou Guang-an

How does one culture 'read' another? In *Literature and Religion*, two scholars, one from China and one from the West, each read texts from the other's culture as a means of dialogue. A key issue in such an enterprise is the nature of religion and what we understand by that term in a world in which ancient religious customs seem to be dying or under threat. Does a comparative study of religious literature offer a way towards mutual understanding – or merely illustrate our differences? Underpinned by their own friendship, these two partners in conversation show what is possible.

'This remarkably adventurous book has become possible because two longstanding friends learned to trust one another. Its readers will find themselves indebted to both the authors for their courtesy to one another and the expectations of care and insight they generate in those willing to embark on comparable studies!'
- **Ann Loades,** Professor Emerita of Divinity, University of Durham, and Honorary Professor in the School of Divinity, University of St Andrews

David Jasper is Emeritus Professor of Literature and Theology at the University of Glasgow, Scotland, and was for many years a Chang Jiang Chair Professor at Renmin University of China, Beijing.

Ou Guang-an is Professor of English Literature and Comparative Literature at the College of Foreign Languages, Shihezi University, China.

Published 2022

Paperback ISBN: 978 0 7188 9619 5
PDF ISBN: 978 0 7188 9628 7